THE HACK'S TALE

THE HACK'S TALE

Hunting the Makers of the Media:
Chaucer, Froissart, Boccaccio

David Hughes

First published in Great Britain 2004

Copyright © 2004 by David Hughes

The moral right of the author has been asserted.

Bloomsbury Publishing Plc, 38 Soho Square, London W1D 3HB

A CIP catalogue record for this book
is available from the British Library.

ISBN 0 7475 4591 X

10 9 8 7 6 5 4 3 2 1

Typeset by Hewer Text Ltd, Edinburgh
Printed in Great Britain by Clays Ltd, St Ives plc

All papers used by Bloomsbury Publishing are natural, recyclable
products made from wood grown in well-managed forests.
The manufacturing processes conform to the environmental
regulations of the country of origin.

For Elizabeth with all my love

Also these pages are offered in homage to those who have helped me write them: to David Reynolds, former director of Bloomsbury, who was as good as his word when promising to commission the book if I could boil down its point to one sentence; his successor Bill Swainson, whose patience and care over the countless sentences that followed have proved a triumph of editorial etiquette; my old friend Paul Sidey for his unremitting support and criticism; John and Nicola Hilton for their welcome in Picardy when Froissart came into the picture; the capital dedicatee who treated me to a cruise of the Aegean that gave me an image of Chaucer's mind; Roger and Görel Wallis for distracting me to their Swedish fastness when I ought to have been off to Italy to chase up Boccaccio; John Burnham Schwartz, my colleague in an unparalleled writers' retreat in Tuscany called Santa Maddalena; Walter Kaiser, genial host of Berenson's library at I Tatti; Bona Frescobaldi for her hospitable glimpse of Boccaccio's Florence; Bernardo Bertolucci who by the happiest of chances entertained me on his film set for an hour or two that furnished a scene of my own; but most of all to Beatrice Monti, vibrant and generous widow of Gregor von Rezzori, whose home in deep woods south-east of Florence, Santa Maddalena, has become one of those paradises about which authors dare only to dream.

CONTENTS

Ye seken lond and see for your winninges,
As wyse folk ye knowen al thestaat
Of regnes; ye ben fadres of tydinges
And tales, both of pees and of debat.
I were right now of tales desolat.
Nere that a marchaunt, goon is many a yere,
Me taught a tale, which that ye shal here.

Geoffrey Chaucer, *The Canterbury Tales*
Prologue To The Man of Law's Tale

Se je disoie: 'Ainsi et ainsi en avint en ce temps', sans ouvrir ne esclarcir la matere qui fut grande et grosse et orrible et bien taillie d'aler malement, ce seroit cronique non pas historiée, et se m'en passeroie bien, se je vouloie; or ne m'en vueille pas passer que je n'esclarcisse tout le fait ou cas que Dieu m'en a donné le sens, le temps, le memoire, et le loisir de cronissier et historier tout au long de la matiere.

Jean Froissart, *Chroniques*

Di racontare cento novelle, o favole o parabole o istorie che dire le vogliamo, raccontate in dieci giorni da una onesta brigata di sette donni et di tre giovani nel pistilenzioso tempo della passata mortalità fatta.

Giovanni Boccaccio, *Decameron*

FOREWORD

This book was sparked off by rage and misery and humour. The rage was directed at the media. The misery was with myself for getting sucked into the maelstrom. The humour was to make it bearable.

I no longer wanted the media swamping my mind, telling me how or what to think, forcing me by their urgency to spend so much time on the vicarious that I was losing grip on the direct. My own life was being sapped. I was being typecast in the mould of everyman, whom the hourly output of word and image set out to influence rather than to inform. They were twisting me round their little finger rather than pointing the way to freedom. This was totalitarianism. It was time to have enough bottle to look at how much of our identity they were stripping us of.

I sat down at home to a close study of the media. Whole mornings were consumed by newspapers. I watched soaps, bulletins, sitcoms, dramadocs. I vastly enjoyed it. Because it was work. The family teased me (I made the mistake of calling it 'research') for inventing an excuse to spend longer hours than usual on magazines and watch even more box, while neglecting my career. The children viewed this as the perfect existence.

All right, I was ready to take the rap for addiction, but not without a struggle. On the principle that in time you root out a problem only by going back to the roots of it, I wondered who started the rot, if I were not myself the culprit.

Any dig into history needed a qualification or two. So I dragged out of storage a high mark in A-level History at KCS Wimbledon, an Oxford degree in English half a century old, an amateur's taste for the past that crept as a guiding force in and out of my novels, a career in journalism that dithered more off than on the fringes of Fleet Street, a short spell writing documentaries on ethnic subjects (Lapps, Icelanders, Gypsies, Swedes) shown by BBC television, a few years scripting feature films in Scandinavia largely about women – all of it muddled together in the liberally concerned and up-to-date mind we are supposed to think we possess.

I thus had rough and ready equipment, if somewhat in need of polishing up, to search out the origins of the media. If obvious mistakes were made, there was bags of room for any reader to enjoy a different take on the argument, such as dismissing it. Besides, in my book, it was never to be an 'argument', just a search. Not much that is regarded as rational has ever struck my mind as reasonable.

At grammar school in Hampshire I read *The Canterbury Tales* by Geoffrey Chaucer (1340–1400) with the instant sympathy of a boy who sees arse spelt as ers under the approving eye of the teacher. At KCS the French master talked of Jean Froissart (1333–1404) as the man who had trapped history in his *Chroniques*, as if the fourteenth century could never have reached posterity without his input. At Oxford a girlfriend reading Modern Languages nudged me into the sexy horseplay of a translation of *Il Decameron*, whose author Giovanni Boccaccio (1313–75) grew into a semblance of a devil when she chose to spend a long vacation in Italy without me.

Half a century later I was now proposing to follow the intertwining paths trod by these three fourteenth-century contemporaries who may or may not have known one another – or indeed be the only quarry in the hunt. There was, as I remembered, plenty of sitcom in Chaucer, who had learnt from Boccaccio and indeed pinched his stories; culture was not in copyright. In stories as neatly cut as screenplays, the gloomy Florentine was not averse to farce with a good sprinkling of sex and violence. It was no surprise that the vernacular led at once to vulgarity. Froissart too wielded an easy French but his purposes were different; nominally a historian, he went about his business asking questions and noting down the answers, so can be cast as a reporter, indeed the first of investigative journalists.

Could I make a case for this trinity being the founding fathers of the media? By nature I detest making cases. All ideas are manic. You pick one at random or it picks you. I just had to get out and about and spot who was responsible for ruining my life as well as giving it infinite pleasure. An idea grabs hold; a writer does his best to make it good. In any case what right had I to talk? I had earned my living out of the media. I dared not work out the amount of paper with my byline on it which I had wasted over half a century without delivering a single discovery of permanence, any insight or passing comfort to my fellow humans, only a modicum of information often slanted, much opinion *ex gratia* disguised as judgment *ex cathedra*, and speculation so slaphappy as to be mistaken for philosophy only by the idle.

So, by paying tribute to three men from the past as well as holding them responsible for my condition of mind, I was making amends by investing more ink and paper in the hope of justifying the reams wasted and the ribbons worn out. Each turned one of western Europe's great languages into grace and slang. Each had taught me to think in the demotic and write in the vernacular. Each in the end had imprisoned me in the media. And all three went on journeys for their life's work: Chaucer to Canterbury and much abroad to France and Italy either fighting a war or on a diplomatic mission, Froissart to much of France and London's royal palaces and beyond to Scotland, Boccaccio to the courts of Naples and as an envoy to Avignon and Brandenburg, and back home to Tuscany.

Thus the concept of travel, like communication, entered into the narrative, but travel more as exploring than as escaping, though the impulses coincided. Was it not fear of the known that sent you racing towards the unknown? My lifetime had taken its good ideas to extremes – radio deafening the ear, telly blinding all day and night, newspapers as thick as holy writ – extremes which were in danger of rendering the human mind senseless by all-too-riveting torture. But that was by the by. If I thought it was as simple as that, I had doubtless missed something even more simple.

Anyway, my men's footsteps, if faint, were there to be followed in. This pilgrimage, conducted alone, only started because of the modest (or perhaps fatal) degree of harm which – along with drinking, smoking, sleeping, eating, ageing – I was persuaded the media were doing me: death of brain cells, narcolepsy, demise of imagination, zapping of independent judgment, attrition of ability to engage at depth in family life, or social activity, or local events that make one feel a wanted member of a vigorous and invigorating society, and love.

That will do for a start.

I WINTER IN LONDON

The start I make is cautious. I look at what I have of Chaucer on the shelf, latching on to that line in an Auden poem, 'a shilling life will give you all the facts'. There is one by A.W. Ward up there, but it was done in 1880, so not in the van of contemporary research. More modern facts are needed. More up to date is a paperback of David Wright's version of *The Canterbury Tales*, out in 1985. He starts off with a brief life to put me in the picture. Only facing the facts gives you the freedom to escape them. I put these two books in a bag, along with shaving tackle, a change of clothes, a notepad and a pen, not forgetting the key to our place in Kent. A passport.

From the house in Lambeth I turn into Walcot Square, where the car is parked, and find a yellow tape barring the way. It flutters in an icy wind. The policeman is no less chilly. He will say only that the crime under investigation is serious, staring at me as though I have committed it. A murder? He eyes me harder. Let's just wait and see, shall we? Till we read all about it in the papers.

Meanwhile the car is under arrest. Within the forbidden area a television truck is drawn up, as if tragedy belongs exclusively to the small screen. So when am I going to get my car back? The copper shrugs shoulders that have matters of life and death on them, as well as a number I memorise.

Look, I'm busy, I've packed, I'm going to Kent, you're putting my project at risk. I avoid saying any of this. Instead I stand staring at the blue back of the law. The lorries pounding down the Kennington Road are getting my blood up. All I want is silence; making my own world down in Kent, settling down to lunch with Chaucer in front of me. But here are the busybody media ignoring anyone outside their cordon of privilege, while my timetable is detained by the police.

As the camera boys smoke and flick butts at my hubcaps, an ambulance backs past the tape, and doors fly open an inch short of a wing mirror of mine. Then drama: a covered body is hurried out on a stretcher. Lenses zoom in. Reporters quickstep for a better view, the doors slam shut, the siren wails.

The yellow tape that delayed my future is removed. I stride to the car, hungry for motion. I slam the door so hard that in the second before ignition fires a fist is pummelling the windscreen. A voice shouts don't move, don't spoil our establishing shot, don't mess up the continuity. I sit at the wheel raging at my obedience to the cameras. Then with a thumbs-up the boys turn their backs.

My life has been put on hold for fifty minutes. They've fined me time. Tonight, losing more precious time at the expense of Chaucer's shilling life, I watch the TV news in Kent. It brings me out in the old London sweat: half-blinded by the daily haze of news and comment in print, on screen, drugged by food and drink to shut it out, fugged by central heating to protect me against its insistent chill, trapped under my own roof in world-wide thickets of bulletins, misted by rumours, foghorned by headlines that are false today and gone tomorrow, I hear nothing on the news about my murder this morning. I go to bed feeling smutty for having tuned in. It all adds to my feeling of being slowly but surely killed.

As a boy I came in at the very end of movable type, when radio was in its infancy and television in the womb. Still well under forty years old, movies were in their youth in my childhood. So I was apt, if not bound, to see the whole proliferation as a responsibility of my lifetime. Lord Reith, who founded the BBC, was only ten years older than my father; Friese-Greene, who first sketched the notion of cinematography, died less than a decade before my birth; the Lumière brothers, who in 1895 opened the first cinema in Lyons and showed the first newsreels, died when I was eighteen and twenty-four respectively; J. L. Baird, who unveiled television in 1926, died at no great age when puberty was busy with me. So, as one who had benefited from their ingenuity and the exploitation that skyhighed as a result, I was ready to pick up the dark side of the tab. The human cost, as newspapers put it.

But I distrusted the idea of forming an obvious thesis out of the above, because it worked against the nature of a pilgrimage being a voyage of discovery. To proceed in a humble spirit, but secretly armed with a lethal theory, spelt failure. It was all likely to end in thin or hot air.

Everything I advanced as a viewpoint (to be avoided like the plague) must be no more necessary to prove true than anything that happened at the behest of external stimuli: this was how we exercised our imaginations. In that exercise existed the pleasure, but also possibly the meaning-if-any, of life. A man who wanted

to put proof of the truth at the end of any such proposition was
already half-dead: QED.

In the morning I enter into the scheme to flush out of hiding the
men of words who beckoned us into the communications
racket, the dads of the media.

   I set up the books in this Kentish house that was built within a
lifetime of Chaucer dying. Nobody knows how old Chaucer
was. In 1345 he might have been in his first year at primary
school or only just born. Ending for sure in 1400, his life spanned
half the Hundred Years War. Depending on your take, he ended
up at sixty which seems old or fifty-five which seems young. A.
W. Ward calls it 'the region of groundless conjecture' – not a bad
phrase for the existence (or not) of a deity. But all these books
wallow in incertitude. Ward, whose first name is Adolphus, has a
fine line in such phrases as 'here it must suffice to risk the
asseveration that . . .' Even Wright has to admit more than once
that 'there is a possibility that he may . . .' A commentator called
D. S. Brewer speaks of Chaucer's life as 'a combination of
vagueness and sharp outline'.

   But then William Blake is saying, 'as Newton numbered the
stars, and as Linnaeus numbered the plants, so Chaucer numbered the classes of men'. And I'm on the right track. 'Every age
is a Canterbury pilgrimage,' Blake asserts; 'we all pass on, each
sustaining one or other of these characters.' The master is giving
me a passport to anyone I want to be.

Across the valley our garden overlooks the Pilgrim's Way. Like
the M20 and Eurostar the southerly route of the pilgrims to
Canterbury is within our view. Becket the blissful martyr stayed

in the next-door palace that is now a farm. Erasmus was our vicar. History is a stroll from the back gate.

For lunch there is shellfish from Griggs of Hythe, who have their boats drawn up on the beach overlooking France, and the wine is from our colony in Bordeaux, wine Chaucer had the job of importing before service to the royals lured him away from the intoxications of trade. Looking at a frosted landscape through single glazing that just about keeps the warmth in, I seek to pin down a shock I first had in boyhood: part and parcel of this pilgrimage.

Aged fifteen I thought I was half in love with Philippa, Chaucer's wife. I associated her in sexiness with someone alive, a grass widow in our Hampshire town, whose naval husband was fighting against the Japanese, though his whereabouts were censored. She was a great big blonde beast of a beauty.

So I'm a lad again and it's wartime and the English teacher tells me the Pilgrim's Way, like fairies, is at the bottom of our garden. For me it's only a short cut from home to class. I squeeze through our hedge, skip a few yards down this hallowed lane, push open the gate into the playing fields and there before me stands a day's boredom encased in Tudor brick – the grammar school.

This old lane eastward leads, however, to Canterbury, a world away, only a few feet wide and dead straight. It runs into deep shadow, the frisson of the foliage is a shiver down the spine, and then in the anarchy of the meadows the spoor is lost. I long to run away into the romance of this great English thoroughfare, which Geoffrey Chaucer made his path to fame.

The teacher can't say where Chaucer's body is, only that his wife Philippa lies entombed in a village nearby. On the map the place looks an easy bike ride. For thrills it's not quite in the class of a sly pedal to the grass widow's bungalow in the hope of watching her undress through an unlikely slit in the blackout curtains, but I'm still keen. The lane winding to the tryst feels nervous. I'm a young knight with a lust that surges beneath the shining armour of his bike.

The woman is on her back. Her body is cut out of white marble. The nose is partly smashed as if someone hit her last night. The hollow eyes flirt out of her skull with the manic emptiness of a girl waiting too long to be asked for a dance. Below the one flared nostril lies the mouth. The lips pout apart. There's a faded card curling beside her saying who she is. A. W. Ward tells me that she married Geoffrey in 1366, and they had two decades of whatever shake-up of bliss and misery was the unique cocktail of their marriage.

I bend over the lips. I stare at the all-too-solid flesh. I see in close-up the dints of smallpox or chisel. The damage on one cheek is wretchedly touching. It would be better to watch today's flesh at the bungalow, but yesterday's armful of the stonily erogenous will do. I almost kiss her. I breathe warmth on the open gasp of those lips. Here lies an ideal, a woman hounded the length of life's road – to end up, not in the fame and worship of Canterbury but less than half known in a village church in Hampshire in a war 600 years on, with only a half adolescent like me to bother pining for her and to see what she might have been like alive.

Back in the town I never do get to grips with the flesh and blood of the naval wife. I hang around the bungalow waiting for blackout restrictions to be lifted or to be asked in. On market days she sits astride a bicycle in the High Street jawing to grown-ups, the mouth rotating as if sucking a gobstopper. I feel the stir below my pelvis. I am too young, born too late.

In London, leaving the newspapers at home, I make it to a C10 bus on the Lambeth Road in good time to catch the 10.18 from Victoria to Lenham. I stare at in-and-out sunshine as we enter Kent on a line I have never used to places I hardly know. A slight fear rocks along with the train. For once I am doing foot-work, walking four miles of the old Pilgrim's Way, wondering if my dicky ankle will hold out.

At Lenham the church is deserted, an outpost of piety visible to pilgrims from the upland path they took to Canterbury. I rise to it, that path. Behind me the town's mood is of lethargic prosperity, the men living in the saloon bars, the women on their nerves. But at the Pilgrim's Way the spirits lift. It has the spring and sponginess of a well-trodden highway which, here and now, has a chance of edging you off the track of the present into the past, if that's where you want to go, and your reasons had better be good. Anyway, the spirit lifts.

With half-closed eyes it's hard to believe any serious change has occurred in six centuries. To build ships and houses, to make room for crops, the trees have gone. The landscape has had a shave.

To the left swell green downs, whitened only by sheep. To the right the Stour valley flashes the white of seagulls against blue sky. A picture painted long ago.

Unzipping against a dry-twigged hedge, I focus on the relief as the eyes blink at the view: a good slash makes the world kin, I am a pilgrim, I am the poet, I am there as well as here. The cloudscape swirls over me then as it does now. The hoofmarks interlock with footprints clodded with horse dung.

Tales are being told above my head.

I plod along not quite hearing. Who is telling the story? Someone is on a palfrey miles up front; I detect only a murmur. And here the convention of storytelling in *The Canterbury Tales* slips conveniently in: people riding at ease on horseback along this survival of a lane, two by two at best, can never have heard the tale, even if shouted at them from the back with a following wind or boomed off the chalk walls of the downs, any more than the storytellers could ease into rhyming couplets when negotiating a network of puddles or wrestling with their material. What nobody is seeking along the Pilgrim's Way is naturalism or even nature.

A rattle disturbs the distance. A metallic shriek of high speed slices the valley as a train of brown and yellow carriages hurtles southwards towards the channel ports. It needs the double-take of a moment to identify this old-fashioned image as the new-style Orient Express. The pilgrims are tramping towards Canterbury. The train is aimed in the direction of the Crusades. It hogs the line. Within the shuddering luxury sit people rich enough to pay for therapy but quaffing wine instead. The snake of train slithers between the fields, trailing behind it a foretaste of abroad.

The tower of Charing church lifts into sight below. A pint of beer beckons, my ankle aches. At the pub I do my sums. Four miles took nearly two hours, so three days for the whole pilgrimage from London to Canterbury makes sense. Very neat. But the calculation is pointless. It fails to allow for the time the stories took to tell, the amount of beer drunk at however many festive stops, a horse's ankle going over amid whinnies of pain; nor does it make room for the sorties to village inns for the night, the couplings on straw that led to being late on parade, the search for a hole to shit in. The whole of the fourteenth century is absent.

Of that time Charing exists as a memento. The Swan stands, bow-windowed, higgledy-piggledy, once a hostelry, now flats. Further up the street the King's Head seems welcoming, then derelict; up for sale, bars dusty with disuse, coaching arch leading to car park half-shut. Pilgrims are no more.

But then a pair of police motorbikes roar down the High Street. Round the church assembles an uneasy gang of youths in dark garb. Their women huddle behind them as black as shadows. They shift and fidget in front of a broken-down palace, where on a gateway from Chaucer's time is pinned a notice not to trespass on private property. Here where the hens strut Henry VIII, on his triumphal way to the Field of the Cloth of Gold, used the banqueting hall round the back to throw chicken bones over his shoulder.

The outriders chug back. Their engines throttle into silence. In a swishy curve a hearse backs towards the gates of the church as if reversing into the past. On the roof the alphabet of lilies names the deceased as Mum. Suddenly Kent is all cockney, it's hop-picking, it's a family funeral, it costs all you've got, it's fallen off a lorry, it's love, and my chest throbs. The coffin is swathed in the best efforts of dozens of florists. Cornish acres are twisted into wreaths. The fields of Holland have been plucked to death.

From the shadows the youths form up like bodyguards. Large men swagger towards the obsequies, men of power in certain pools of East End backwaters, huge sentimental men with respect not only for the defunct but for money and violence. This afternoon London has invaded Kent in black to bury one of its rare matriarchs. A resentment of death's criminality pervades the afternoon. They all vanish into a fourteenth-century church taken over by stealth. They too are repeating history.

On the train back, irresistibly, I open the *Kentish Express*. The fast rail link to France has thrown the locals into disarray. Their homes will lose value. Sixty pages follow of anaemic news. They are the same old stories.

At Victoria the *Evening Standard* posters announce that London hospitals are to merge or to close. The bus passes the dozens of lit screens above the foyer of Channel 4 in Horseferry Road. They are all dispensing with a flicker the same something. At home I am in good time for the BBC's 6 o'clock news, in which Premier and President are meeting in Washington to discuss launching against an eastern country what a Russian leader describes as a third world war.

Moreover a new disease has been created, springing from implants in breasts; probably few are immune. To crown it all they are wondering in some Latin country whether to exhume a man buried with a lottery ticket in his best suit. He has won the jackpot.

I turn off the set. I will forget these items in an hour. I have neither the obligation nor the need to know. They will confuse progress along the Pilgrim's Way. They trump up a drama lacking in the events, leaving in the mind's evening a passive blank as smooth as a large gin but with nothing like the kick.

I spend an early hour in Kennington skimming my memory of Chaucer's sixty years.

During a seven-year blank in modern knowledge of his movements, the early 1360s, he was fined two shillings for assaulting a Franciscan friar in Fleet Street, and just the thought of a cleric passing El Vino is enough to link this abrupt moment of tipsy youth with Chaucer's daily pitcher of wine granted a few years later by John of Gaunt. The association will give El Vino's house claret a special savour at my next visit, as if Chaucer had imported it. Not far away in Vintry the future poet helped out his dad in the shop by selling wine over the counter.

Again, in the rooms Chaucer occupied rent-free above the Aldgate, as often as not he was at his quiet desk. But one day in 1381 when he was fortyish he gazed down to witness hordes of the unwashed jamming the gateway below his loft, on their riotous way to bearding the teenage King Richard II at Smithfield – yes, the Peasants' Revolt, as unrepeatable a catch in the breath of history as St Paul's Cathedral's breathtaking survival in 1940 of the devastation that ringed it with fire when I was ten.

As Clerk of the King's Works the poet was in charge of erecting scaffolds for a couple of tournaments at Smithfield, just up the road from El Vino or a cross-city stroll from Aldgate, receiving from Richard II an annual butt of wine in 1397, two years before he leased a house in the gardens of Westminster Abbey, where at the weekend our son is picked up from school. Here in October 1400, with the cloisters to pace in thought, an eccentric priesthood to furnish his mind with yet another set of tales, and over half a century of his lease to expire, he died.

A quarter of an hour from home in Kennington in Borough High Street, where at the Tabard the first page of *The Canterbury Tales* is set, a library devoted to local history is run by an enthusiast who for virtue and humour might have got his name on the cast list for the Prologue. He lays out for me a large-scale plan of fourteenth-century London: a simplified version of the current *A to Z*. The Borough Market is in place, but the Stewes, marked as fishponds but in fact brothels, have gone.

In Chaucer's time these seamy streets have thronged for half a century with whores exiled by law from the City of London. The map sketches a patchwork of pubs and pillories, ale-houses, ranks of taverns for wine, the hovels of widows who make a groat serving rough food. The Abbot of Hyde's Inn, otherwise known as the Tabard, is close to where the George now stands, the one remaining pub that looks faintly like the house where Chaucer lay that night, making friends and comments with the same deft ambiguity.

I drink a pint of 6X in the courtyard of the George. The bubble panes in the windows look period – in a word, faked. The uneven run of galleries, good for nipping to and from bedchambers belonging to others, gives a kitsch sketch of the old Tabard, at least for a tourist. The clink of glasses inside is immemorial. It's the sound of pilgrims gathering.

I can walk no further into the story until I face up to this right ankle I hurt again walking the Pilgrim's Way. Specialists have looked at its rugose bulge. At upwards of a hundred pounds a time they advise me to try trainers or seek help elsewhere.

The ankle enjoys it in bed. Sheets shut it up. It likes plenty of newspapers. A good book will keep it quiet for hours. When I get home from an arduous lunch the ankle tells me I need to keep it up, preferably on a sofa. Nobody knows why it gets painlessly drunk in the evenings, except as an alternative to the chemical niagara that pours through my system. Nor does anyone tell me why the ankle has suddenly let me down.

Meanwhile the media are its one comfort.

Why not give in to the media? I live in their midst – after all, I live in the modern mode. The four storeys of our house contain the following devices that make sure our lives function at speed: 4 telephones, 3 televisions, 1 fax, access to the Internet thrice, 2 digital cameras, 3 PCs, 4 radios including an all-night earpiece, 4 cellphones, email, text message, not to mention such wilier instruments of communication as a grand piano, a clarinet, 4 guitars, a clutch of recorders, and half a dozen broken-down typewriters dating from the prehistory of electronics.

All the more potent of these inventions think they are in charge of us, dawn to dusk, all night long, for good. I brood on the picture of a household like ours, or a mind like mine, in which every world event, passing fashion, or nothing at all, is momentously momentarily happening with every ring of the phone or slap of a letter on the mat or the blessed silence of an email. Future and past are fighting it out with the present in room-to-room warfare.

Back to the joint with a life of its own, I have to make capital out of it. The ankle slows me down to another sense of time. I used to quicken towards a date. Now I ease to the rendezvous, in unfamiliar pain, oddly not myself, borrowing time belonging to someone else. I decide to be more like the fourteenth century I'm in. I treat my disorder as a stand-in for illness then: a victim of the plague with a single day to live, a bystander on one leg and a crutch.

But when did the media start? It must have been when the first word was formed, when a human voice uttered an intelligible sound, when the cave stopped echoing with pre-barbarian protobabble.

The experts defined it as a communicative shift – 'a radical change in the technology and practice of communication' – when at ever-shortening intervals the personal way of getting your meaning across altered its techniques. That posited a medium that led to media. Speech.

Four huge changes were on record. The time intervals between these shifts were oddly consistent. Fifty-five thousand or so years ago there was the move to speech. Vast gap. Then the written cipher or rune or word came into play about 5,500 years ago. Long interval. As of now it was 550 years since print by movable type was invented. Short pause. Currently on-screen language has been with us for little more than fifty-five years. If the logic is pleasing, it is also meaningless. Time could never be measured in years; nor did progress have the wit to be other than accidental.

Bodily change started this march of the media. The organs meant to breathe and eat and drink got evolution into their system. The throat fathered a larynx. The lungs expanded to serve any need from rhetoric to abuse. Trying the voice out, flexing the muscles of speech, getting your point over, must have sounded like babel for millennia until the light in someone's eye told you she had understood. That was when the grunt of copulation softened into murmurs of love. Homo sapiens started to care and argue. Ego began to make sense, as it developed sounds that betokened rage, selfhood, greed, sex, drowsiness, jealousy, avarice: versions of the seven prime needs that developed into the deadly sins. Good media men in the making, these primitive orators passed on to their as yet dumb children the standards which the invention of language enabled them to share.

The coming of language also trained memory. It packed the spaces of the mind with matters, both practical and poetic, to be passed on by recital and repetition to coming generations. A culture formed, of which as yet there was no legible trace: literally all in the mind. How much more potent must myth be when issued from the tongues of men rather than the pages of books. Each man was a god to his offspring. He spewed forth wisdom, he uttered mystery, he created the child's world in words. Thus for thousands of years the encyclopaedia of world knowledge remained oral.

Then came writing.

In cuneiform the Sumerians noted their day-to-day dealings in commerce. Three centuries before Christ, with an eye to efficiency but with undertones of power, the government, in societies as farflung as China, India and Egypt, took over writing as the weapon of record: the law, the exchequer, the state, all grew in strength and wealth on this tide of literacy. The elite wrote themselves into history; the illiterate were ruled into oblivion. Meanwhile the old storytellers still ignored the written word; their brand of power sprang from intoxicating their hearers with the rhythmic beat of words that passed as regularly as heartbeat from a long line of forebears. It was of their skills and methods that long afterwards both Chaucer in his *Canterbury Tales* and Boccaccio in *The Decameron* took advantage: they unnoddingly used Homer's method of passing on a story by mouth only to a mixed audience.

I turn a room in our house in Kennington into a nerve centre from which to conduct the campaign.

I strip the room of most of the equipment mentioned earlier, all the electronics. I just want to use my hands on this job. So I set out the pens, looking for one I can fill with real ink, but the rubber of the sac has perished. I pick over the old typewriters. My father's Regent portable (*c.* 1930, as old as I am) has one key broken and needs a refit.

From *Yellow Pages* I run to ground one firm round the corner in Southwark, half a mile away, which still deals in such ware. I heave up the big office Olympia too, on which I hammered out the weekly pieces for the press that gave me just enough to live on but too much trouble to live with. Looking at the heavy grey monstrosity of this object, as Teutonic as a tank, I regret the hours I spent pounding it in search of fame and funds, if not (in brackets) truth, and wonder if I have the nerve, let alone the energy, not to mention the cash, to get it repaired.

Meanwhile I get maps at the geography shop in Petty France SW1. I see at once that Chaucer's pilgrims took the northern way, starting due east from the Tabard. The places named in the text are so few that they leap off the page. 'Lo, Depeford, and it is half wey pryme', as the pilgrims stagger to a halt. 'Lo, Grenewych, ther many a shrewe is inne', and drinks are taken. As for 'Lo! Rouchestre stant heere faste by!', the pilgrims are bedding down at Rochester, while after 'I come to Sidenbourne' another night is spent at Faversham, and perhaps a third in the unidentified Bobbe-up-and-doun, probably a bluff called Harbledown on the modern map, before descending upon the shrine at Canterbury on bended knees.

The bit I walked from Lenham the other day was on the southern route starting at Winchester, still mostly farms in a silence broken only by a grumble of motorway. But of the original pilgrims' route from London little will be found to have survived, save perhaps a few feet of one footpath on the outskirts of a suburb of an overdeveloped town that was once a community.

It is time I read the master again. Where is he? In some place I have the great and good Skeat edition (1894) of the whole of Chaucer in seven volumes, bound so thickly in heavy Victorian cloth and boards that it strains the biceps to hold them above the knee. Each volume looks as authoritative as a Holy Bible on a small lectern in a miniature cathedral. The footnotes are a crypt of hidden secrets beneath every page.

I bought it a third of a century ago in Petersfield, in a bookshop too lazy to change its prices as inflation crept up, so you could dig bargains out of the backward dust of the shelves. It was marked nine guineas the set. Guineas? We were already decimal. I counted out the cash. I hurried the bargain off in my arms. I tumbled it into the car before anyone twigged. Not seven miles from the Pilgrim's Way of my boyhood, I set it up on a mantelshelf in Hampshire under an Epstein drawing of a nude. I had found a source of life.

Over the years I changed my domestic arrangements too often to remember where Chaucer has gone. Everything but instant laundry was too heavy for the suitcases that twisted my arm at airports as I shuttled across the ocean from one flat in London to an apartment in New York, as one decade propped up the next. Everywhere I left behind the suits that others were soon to wear, the manuscripts that might prove masterpieces if only I still had them to work on, the mirrors I once looked good in, the cameras that snapped everything except aspects of myself, the emptiness that then defined me.

Chaucer is quite hard to hide. His seven volumes are unlikely

to have been burned. They are neither subversive nor inflam-
matory. The complete works left Hampshire with me when in
the 1970s I settled in London within a quarter-mile of the
Tabard. A year later I moved abroad, under yet another dis-
locating load of suitcases. Is Chaucer still in the South of France?
I see the volumes gathering the gritty dust of the garrigue blown
in by the mistral, in the tawny sunlight that entered a small
window in a silk-worm barn of a library. A house had stood on
this spot since Caxton first printed Chaucer a century after he
died. It was so sublime as to be ridiculous. In all its beauty this old
farm had fewer facilities than all the Middle Ages put together.

My ex-wife, who after our separation moved north into the
Ardèche, is dead. I call her son in Spain. As to a defective he
explains that the house he inherited from his mother, which is
proving hard to sell, contains scattered on the floor of an upper
room, unrestored at the time of her decease, a mass of books,
damp encrusted and heat curled from extremes of temperature,
which might belong to me. I am fond of him and I mention
Chaucer.

He is busy teaching ecology in Barcelona. As a schoolboy the
lad used to lean against the seven pillars of Skeat's Chaucer on
the mantelshelf in Hampshire under that Epstein nude and air his
rebellious opinions about press barons and television tycoons.
He is shortly driving to the Ardèche to hunt out buyers. Sensing
urgency in the air, he suggests an immediate date for me to join
him.

It seems I have left a lot of property in France. He thinks it
might benefit from being packed in black binliners and conveyed to a cemetery of my own choice. The lure of the trip
excites me. I now think of France as a little-known territory

where Chaucer was first imprisoned and I first escaped a marriage. His English was more like French than my French ever was but less like the language of Froissart. All of it still looks pidgin on the page.

A budget airline flies me to Nîmes for a tenner; the communications go on improving, while communicating gets its lines crossed. My stepson and I drive north through memories of the Languedoc into the chill that surrounds my ex-wife's widowed house, her desk awaiting tomorrow's work, the air of a purgatory in stasis.

Yes, my books are all over the floor in heaps, the paperbacks bending over backwards to look damp and lost. Nibbled bindings are fertilised with tiny pellets of shit where mice have been wolfing culture. It all cries out for a rescue I haven't the heart or the money to bring to it.

I am after a single quarry. Only in the study, at second glance, shelved with Jung and Strindberg and sets of even more neurotic moderns, do I find in due order the seven fat spines of Skeat's unspeakably missed and valued edition of the works of Geoffrey Chaucer – not just a book, not even seven mere books, but a lifetime's work for two men, the author and the editor centuries apart. Never have I so much relished owning an object or felt in my hands such an entity or been so pleased to be living in a present where such things from the past exist.

Amid all this triumph a nudge in the mind tells me to look for Chaucer's friend (how well they knew each other is anyone's guess) the chronicler Jean Froissart (the first of the great reporters), whom Chaucer meets on at least one of his northern French journeys through land then as wild as this stretch of the

Midi is now. Of Froissart I had once possessed only a classroom selection. I have no image of a face on a page.

At Nîmes no excess baggage is charged for Chaucer. The fare home is just £1.94 plus airport tax. The world is nuts and also bananas, which is what I have for lunch aboard. I carry my designer shoulder-bag under my left arm so as to put no strain on my right ankle. It has *The Canterbury Tales* in it; the rest of the œuvre I have risked to the hold in a holdall. As they rise into the air six volumes sink well below freezing.

I make a point of not reading an English newspaper on the flight home. It will make no sense after France. In any case my appetite for the staples of all the columns – controversy, murder, failure of public services, failure of private lives, rape, injustice, invasion, intrigue, perversion, scandal – has diminished to nil after a gratifying meal with Louis. The whole of France plus its family sat around us in the state of hebdomadal rapture that is Sunday lunch in the provinces.

I am home. *Troilus and Criseyde* in their original spelling have survived the arctic air thousands of feet above France. So have Skeat's cool notes. Only *The Canterbury Tales*, which I fingered in the plane over a tiny imitation of a pitcher of claret, still feel as warm as blood when we get to Stansted. I crack open a volume and put my nose into the nineteenth century in all its musty weight, taking its time to reach back hundreds of years to make the fourteenth century ring true. It's not shut up in books unless you want it to be. Off the pages comes the stink, the plague, the unknowingness, the hectic belief in a god far crueller than the one we may or don't believe in now, the viciousness on earth and the bad taste in heaven. Out of the verse emerge the humours of a time in which every human challenge was intolerable, when you were bound to come worst out of whatever gamble you took.

The dark was a hidden knife. Daylight was a drunken effort to avoid the dark. You were someone else's. No one belonged to himself, not even a king: royalty was the property of assassins. Not often had the spirit any time to break out of servitude and spur you on. You were going to catch the next contagion, be stripped like a house, burnt like a book, hung like game, drawn like meat, quartered like a crucifix. You cannot win even if everyone else is losing. The food is no good, the drink sour.

Yet Chaucer found his century not unamusing. He brought to it his own burlesque of dignity, sweetened with fun, salted by happiness. Few of these qualities are obvious on landing at Stansted.

For days I guzzle Chaucer. I take his pentameters in gulps. I long to read the whole man at a sitting. I have the time. I make it for myself by declining to take on any other work or play until I master his universe.

As always the key that unlocks it is to identify. A duplicitous simplicity in Chaucer's genial eye makes it easy to be at one with everybody, even the villains and rogues, in particular the women. In the 'Prologue' to *The Canterbury Tales* the poet teases out the essentials of the 'nyne and twenty' pilgrims in a few lines, with not a wasted touch. You see aspects of yourself in them all; each of us is an amalgam of 'sondry folk, by aventure y-falle in felawshipe'. On the surface I had the manners of the Knight – 'of his port as meke as is a mayde, he never yet no vileinye ne sayde in all his lyf, un-to no maner wight' – but I was like that only in part. Under the skin, I perceived, I was as 'hot' as the Summoner, 'and lecherous, as a sparwe' and coarse in my tastes: 'wel loved he garleek, oynons, and eek lekes, and for to drinken strong wyn, reed as blood'. Like the Reeve I had my mean and cunning side which rarely went on show. A pleasure in food put me in touch with the Cook, despite his untoothsome habit of boiling chicken with the marrowbones. I could see eye to eye with the Man of Law, 'nowher so bisy a man as he there nas, And yet he semed bisier than he was'. From the moment of first seeing the sea I had wanted to be the Shipman and share the hazards of tides and currents under the moon.

A 'fadre of tydinges and tales, bothe of pees and of debat', as the Man of Law puts it, Chaucer enables me to know at once that I was born not to feel confusion or suffer nerves or doubt or succumb to horror or hollowness, but to understand. His lines still sound like private conversation meant for just your ear, instead of showing off to impress or suppress you. Yet there is no character in any TV show or film or sitcom who owes nothing to, or has improved upon, this parade of human quality, vanity, sin, crime, self-delusion: you can save watching a year's television by reading the 'Prologue' in an evening. It contains and expands the rumours, and humours, of all life in 858 lines. I hardly exaggerate.

But nobody starting out on their own pilgrimage, to whatever shrine, needs a better or swifter education in humanity. The very words fizz with novelty because they are old; our own tongues reach back to them, our minds excavate their exact meanings from the time they were current in accents local, Scouse, Brum, Geordie, the rough ways of talk long before the hoity-toity of the Home Counties started getting the sound of Chaucer, if not the meaning, all wrong.

★   ★   ★

But did Chaucer himself ever undertake the pilgrimage to Canterbury? Perhaps he only (only?) invented it. At home in Aldgate, taking a swig from his daily pitcher, he makes it up as he goes along by not going along. For hundreds of years, though, thousands of others do put their feet where their faith is, drawn to Becket's shrine by the cheapness of a night's lodging (1 penny) even if the hire of a horse costs two shillings.

Today I am on my own pilgrimage. The day dawns on the A2 after the turn-off to Canterbury. Due to catch the 10 a.m. catamaran from Dover, I am in a tizzy lest we come late, or drive into the wrong lane, or the weather cause a delay, or the ferry be overbooked. It is no good anyone saying that cross-Channel traffic was subject in the fourteenth century to more hazardous imponderables. This is the neurosis of now, and this is me living it.

Aboard I am on my own but among dozens of others on the same mission, puffily emphasising their obesity by bulges of clothes, already downing the ritual of the day's first drink. For of course this has every mark of a pilgrimage. We have faith in what we are off to buy, we who worship booze, we who cannot get enough of our belief in it. Nobody in the vessel looks as though he follows any of the callings of Chaucer's band. Nuns, friars and manciples are not to the fore. But old English features still figure: a ruddiness of cheek, blue eyes too wide to be anything but wicked, a joviality that rises above anorak and trainer in this loungeful of jeans, a respectability gone to pot, an honesty not put to the test, a self-interest that will melt into generosity at a touch − niceness. But they also look an ugly gang, do my compatriots, out for pillage if not rape.

Beyond Calais lie the great empty sweeps of the autoroutes,

writing off every town in or out of sight. I am invading this bare country to secure its wine. I eat up the miles to the restaurant, one of those proud, well-run servants of the bourgeois that prosper on byways up and down France. I order foods basic to all times and peoples in our appetising West: *moules*, *entrecôte*, *fromage*, *vin*, they require neither translation nor excuse. The mastery of well-being of which France is the mistress eases into the marrow of my bones. It is like being plunged into intensive care when in the best of health.

Down a valley strung with villages that escaped most of two world wars lies the main square of Hesdin, where I am to buy French wine but from a British business: the Wine Society has a corner shop. It is Edward III all over again: his fight in the Hundred Years War, among issues less civilised, was to keep Bordeaux for English tables and palates. From a girl at the desk, the murmur of a smile you see in understated French films greets me. A manicured finger taps in my share number. I am recognised by machine. I can buy what I like with no tax to speak of. I choose a claret or two, white burgundy, some deep red from the south, don't be greedy. Within seconds a dozen cases are being loaded into the back of the car, while Hesdin snoozes into the non-event of an afternoon.

Suddenly, off one of those straight roads that cut their length through the solitariness of France, Agincourt is half a mile to the right. The wine chinks in the boot as I brake. What's this? It's a battle long after Chaucer's time. Froissart was dead when he could have written an account of it. This detour will put the return ferry at risk. But Henry V, though out of period, talks me into it.

A lane quietly corkscrews through the village, spelt Azincourt.

At every turn roadside cut-outs of outsize medieval warriors aim their arrows or flaunt their chain mail. They are as garishly two-dimensional as the past itself. A modern museum resembling a bad design for a chapel repels any desire to visit it. Well out of the tourist trap of the village itself, the ground rises slightly and a mile or more on there is an orientation plan that surveys the battlefield. All that is boring of France stretches as far ahead as the eye cannot bear to see.

At first my car draws up alone, but not for long. Within seconds several French cars zoom in and tumble out their passengers. I feel under attack. They are in suits and wear hats. Their rimless glasses gleam. I catch the idea of revenge lurking in their race memory. Expecting at any moment an explosion of the hostility that still smoulders between our nations, I retreat along a lane that cuts through the heart of the battlefield. Unbounded agriculture now occupies it. The spaces without a hedge in sight are still a graveyard for 10,000 French knights who, once unhorsed, were too heavy on their feet to fight. English bones too pass under our wheels, the British tyres a bit bulgy from the weight of French wine the Saab is carrying in the boot.

On the ferry they drink, read papers and paperbacks, and drink. I think of the last stage that revolutionised the media: the alphabet, communication's A to Z, coming into play. What next? Writing started as a species of shorthand, notes scratched on stone, indented in clay, scrawled on papyrus. But a proper text needed more accuracy and extent, so there developed more than a thousand years before Christ a convention of up to thirty signs which, in whatever language, visually echoed the sounds that the brain commanded the voice box to utter by means of tongue, palate, teeth and lips. Scribes tended to be regarded with awe. They were credited with recording not only state secrets but the mysteries of the universe. Often immured in religious houses, they were the only people with the time and silence to make sure that communication could now occur between people who were miles or countries apart.

Next came printing.

At once this stroke of genius, supposedly invented by the goldsmith Johannes Gutenberg in 1450, turned 'scripture' secular. It mechanised literature, putting the printed word into the hands of anyone who could decipher it. Scholars ceased to hold exclusive rights to the culture; the day of the general reader had dawned. As a superior vehicle, the limousine of medieval law and diktat, Latin hardly survived this super-change, as printing everywhere swung behind the vernacular, including the relative slang in which Chaucer, Froissart and Boccaccio had written their masterworks within the preceding century. Of the first-named author, William Caxton alone published two editions. Anyone who signed his name with anything but a cross now knew who Chaucer was. The arrival of hot metal also standardised spelling and syntax; proofs were there to be corrected. The premodern world was in our midst.

Returning to London in the dark on the A2, the Pilgrim's Way is invisible except in the lines of the street lamps on the outskirts of towns. On today's trip I came quite close to Crécy, which battle Froissart did report, though not as an eyewitness. There is lots more of the past that hasn't happened yet in my present either. I know this for a prime reason: all day I have been free of the media. With relief I do not know what is happening anywhere in the world, except to me – until I see the lit oblongs of the slatted hoardings in the Old Kent Road advertising in sequence an insurance company, an alcopop, a television spectacular.

I have been at sea. It is possible to achieve almost anything within twenty-four hours if you refuse to take time seriously or even into account. Or listen to anyone else. I am well and truly on the way home.

What more happened to Chaucer? Nothing, or not much that is on record. He kept himself to himself. He fostered a low profile. The books I flick through are no help. They keep informing me how little is known. Even old Skeat, not to mention the later Robinson, seems rather to relish the certainty that only a few portraits of his subject are known, and those in the margins of manuscripts. Skeat may well be deriving a secret pleasure from the totality of his knowledge. He suspects the future can discover nothing to dent his omniscience. We all long to know all life. Yet the more facts there are, as in an evening of television, the less they cohere or count.

I look at the maps for the next step.

We are in Southampton. In 1350 it was a tight-packed walled city on an inlet of the Solent. Within it as an adolescent I am staying in an old house in Bugle Street with my friend, a journalist on the *Southern Daily Echo*, who infects me with the lure of his trade. The office reeks of printer's ink. Old men in aprons move at seemly speed, dangling to the floor long proofs of words fresh from the typewriter. Younger men laze at desks with big black telephones to their ear, taking down on copy paper yet more words by hand. Presses clatter and by the time we're back from a beer and a sandwich the street corners of the city are shouting out all those words, the pubs are full of them, the trams alive with their clamour. I feel their power in me thrumming like the presses printing them. I too shall report events. I too must have my say about the ways of the world.

As a boy Chaucer was educated in Southampton.

His father John, being a vintner, was here appointed deputy to the King's Butler. That meant Edward III drank good wine on the eve of yet another marauding raid on France to defend his supplies of claret. This job rewarded John Chaucer for attending the King in Flanders in 1338. Ten years later he was collecting duty on imported cloths in certain ports. It is hopeless to look in Southampton for a trace of Chaucer, except on the saltwater fringes. They have shifted only an inch or two in these oceans of time since the fourteenth century. I pick up shells like those he might have listened to. There are pebbles only a touch more smooth than they were then.

But where do these not half-literal traces get you? I am in Southampton, yes, and in boyhood, what's more, and I ache to write for the evening paper like my friend, and I am looking for the seeds of the language I have to write in, and at school I am being taught French and English in more or less equal measure, but have to find my own tongue. With effort, with an effort that looks like ease, we will get neater, and nearer to things. We will come close to Chaucer. He is still there.

By the time I give up going to Southampton, still seduced by the tendency of journalism to elevate a man into a voice if not a celebrity, I am in London. So is Chaucer. He is back in London headquartered in Vintry, home of the wine trade. At seventeen he is a page to Prince Lionel. Nepotism forces him to attend great occasions. He meets the right people. John of Gaunt comes his way. Is he by now already collecting material or only autographs?

In 1359 he is off with the army to France in another twist or turn of the Hundred Years War, no doubt thinking: I can use this drama to write up a battle scene. But he's caught at Reims. No evidence exists as to how he is treated in captivity. He leaves no protest in writing; his rights seem not to have come into the equation. No doubt his scars lie between the lines of his work and may in due course be stripped bare by psychiatry. I doubt if he thinks his sufferings derive from anything but the incurability of life.

In 1360, the year of his ransom, Chaucer is back in France. Has he caught our chic urge to cross the Channel at any cost? Or is someone twisting his arm? Anyway the general mood is of hope. This spring a huge peace is signed at tiny Brétigny, a hamlet near Chartres, and from thereabouts Chaucer carries letters to England.

Calais was the port of embarkation. He spends days there, as Caesar did, buffeted by wind, staring at turbulence. The wood of fragile barks creaks noisily against the timber of quays at each sickening wave. Lots of them wait: knights, squires, cooks, shipmen, merchants, kicking their heels, drinking as the only way of dumbing time, telling stories as crude as boasts.

In another party Froissart turns up, seeking passage to England. Neither he nor his fellow author has written a word, but as young men will they exchange glances if they see each other at all: putative rivals to putting their century in focus, passing on the facts to a future they cannot see as other than unimaginable? The seas calm. They may not be on the same ship, only part of the same fleet.

This French trip in 1360 was paid by Lionel, so Chaucer was still in his service, a fact that has the fatigued smack of what schoolboys forget and quiz-show wizards remember. Of far more concern, as earlier mentioned, is the void of six years that followed. From 1361 Chaucer vanishes from history. Lionel is a viceroy in Ireland, but there is no suggestion our friend accompanied him into those green mists.

And does Chaucer love Philippa? How does love feel in that century? I want more for the Chaucers. I want them to be struck in the breast by desire and destomached with love. That's what I want Geoffrey and Philippa, daughter of Sir Payne Roet, sister of Katharine Swynford, later to be the third wife of John of Gaunt, to be feeling for each other. To sit at an oak table, heads together, and itch and fidget and giggle and eat from their fingers and dribble drink into each other's mouth; in the interests of a poetry and a language and a truth that are only just starting up, it's lust, it's a lusty love, it's lovely and lustful, and I hope it is happening at a pitch of romance that has no cut of the cynical to it. Even dear old Skeat cannot gainsay me in his footnotes or confirm – he wouldn't dare for fear of shocking the nineteenth century out of its boots.

Eight years of marriage, and John of Gaunt comes up with a stipend for them both. Geoffrey still gets his daily pitcher of wine. A pitcher is as deep as a piece of string is long. We do not know the location of their lodging or mansion, but it's somewhere in London. Philippa and Geoffrey have a child called Thomas.

Back in the Borough, not far from the Tabard, I catch sight of a charity shop and wonder why I think it matters. A rank of frocks hangs over a pile of paperbacks that nudges a variety of ornaments. I know without admitting it what my mind is toying with. Last year a niece on her twenty-first lifted all Cumbria to dizzy heights of transvestite invention by asking everyone to a dance in the identity of their dreams or in the worst of drag.

I grew a moustache for the occasion. Having suppressed a lifelong wish to be a death-dealing dictator I chose to be General Pinochet, using an outmoded double-breasted suit to trim my paunch, assuming an aggressive look when anyone young appeared to be enjoying the party. They were gracious enough to congratulate me for verisimilitude. Tomorrow, as youth awakens to hangovers, they will find themselves in the concentration camp of my disapproval. Fat chance. By morning I shall be having scrambled eggs for breakfast as very much myself or anyone else.

But the seed was sown at that party.

I walk into the shop. Local matrons man it. One room is hung with clothes in diminished light. Only my fingers can tell by texture what I am looking at. I feel my chin, as rough as serge. I can be bearded by the middle of next week. What I am up for, keen on, attracted by the daring of, is decking myself out like Geoffrey Chaucer. In these glum regions of charity, away from the ladies, I shift between the garments in quest of a smock. It has to feel right, have puffy sleeves and a tight wrist, and needs to swing like a skirt below the genitals. For of course all these half-hidden clothes are female. And then indeed I do find – I know it at once – the right garb, a long, crudely woven dress with a high collar and an ample waist that would fit any woman without an hourglass figure.

I pick it off the hook, hold it to the bulb, snatch at the curtain,

stand in private, trouserless, and enter the garment head first. It
wriggles down my body like someone interfering with me. I
look into a cracked mirror. If the stubble is not yet up to the
mark, and I lack headgear, I'm as good as a fourteenth-century
poet. I need stockings too, and the idea of the thrill of them
unfolding up my legs is stirring enough to induce me to ask the
ladies whether they have any. Their answer is guarded. They tell
me that underwear is rather too 'secondhand' an item for them
to display, unless I care to look into the 'ragbag'.

The study door in Kennington has an unfitting lock. I wait to
conduct my experiment until everyone goes out or to sleep. The
portraits of Chaucer lie open on the desk. I think him. He wakes
early. Dawn is to come. A London skyline of chimney pots is
only just touched in. There will be trouble today. A foreign trip
looms in all its chicanery and risk. Pirates haunt the mouth of the
Thames to evade duty at my docks. I rise naked. I draw a thick
stocking up one thigh, then reflect on my standing at court
which might be plummeting, and pull the next stocking on. My
legs feel agreeably constricted by sexual charge. I am cross-
dressed with the fourteenth century.

In a flash of understanding, more willed than likely, I know
that he is wearing nothing round his hips, his privates hang loose,
and all I need do is throw the charity smock over my shoulders
and let it fall free. I stand without a mirror, reflected only by my
narcissistic feeling that I am right, because this sense of an
awakening other, this gathering sense of a new day dawning,
is so far from myself.

I cannot bring myself to walk about the Borough dressed as
Chaucer, even in enlightened times. So armed with a mental
image of myself thus attired, plus a full-length polaroid taken in

the mirror which not only the anachronism of the camera held in my fingers renders ridiculous, I go for lunch to the Boot & Flogger.

This early wine bar, founded in the 1960s, is encased in attitudes as old-fashioned as the panelling, lit by candles, festive with noise. Here the past has been picked up at auction: big brown barrels, old bells on spiral springs transplanted from the service kitchen of an inn, blackboards with the day's specials squeaked out in chalk. It is the best yet double of the Tabard. Anyway, my idea of Chaucer likes it, and that serves.

At the next table laughter volleys back and forth. The board bears several empty bottles. Other revellers arrive at the feast. More tables are moved together. In good English tradition, a motley crowd gathers round mine host, a caricature cockney who has made good, an empurpled face proving it. I gaze covertly.

The pilgrims assemble. They are as solemn as idiots. The talk is of racing and fortunes made and lost, of motors and high-speed pile-ups, of women dropped and picked up. A sage with the look of a street-trader raises a digit for a bottle of a finer claret. His prosperity must have fallen off a lorry. A coronary or two look imminent. Aloof from the table a girl with big eyes poised over sensual lips pouts in slow motion and mid-air, as if kissing herself in a mirror. Behind her ferally sits a weighty greybeard in rimless glasses, mouthing the rouge of the wine over his tongue. Chaucer suggests to me that she might be one of the whores down at the Stewes on her day off.

The men are engaged in the unsteady pastime of putting the world to rights. I hope to be invited on whatever pilgrimage they plan, while staying unnoticed. But they are a gang. As convinced a loner as the poet, I work my way through a glass of claret and a black coffee, while hiding behind the media: the newspapers from the rack are an unreadably good disguise. Chaucer shares everything with me except the coffee and the papers. For him neither exists.

The girl rises with an air of sinuous boredom and moves off towards the lavatory. All over the Tabard glances follow her curves like slaves. Chaucer makes a note. I can use her. I can turn her into someone, a nun or prioress ('that of hir smyling was ful simple and coy'). She is the hint I have been looking for. By no means was I wasting my time today when I dropped into the Boot & Flogger mentally dressed as a poet. I raise the last swig of claret to the polaroid of me in medieval drag which I pull from my pocket just as the bill comes and she as spry as the Wife of Bath – 'bold was hir face, and fair, and reed of hewe' – comes back from the lavatory and, a miracle, smiles at me in collusion as I lower the newspaper.

I race off into Borough Market. It smells of earth. The viaducts that cross it hammer and grind with trains. Their electrics make the past fizz. I might just catch up with Chaucer. He is only just out of sight. A dealer switches his light bulb off in a portacabin hung with garlic, ginger from Costa Rica, stalls piled with Jamaican bananas, Spanish cauliflower, apples from France and melons from Israel. I pass the cathedral, once the priory of St Mary Overie which owned the fish ponds if not the brothels. A likeness of Chaucer's friend Gower, whom he teased in light verse, lies within on an elaborate tomb, looking highly coloured in death.

Walking over London Bridge, waves lapping at the foot of stone stairs, I am moving back to the heart of the city where

Chaucer lives. Halfway across the bridge on the eastern side projects the ghostly site of the chapel to Thomas à Becket, who had by his murder set afoot the whole idea of a pilgrimage to his shrine. So he too had his responsibility in helping the media on their way. I now tear up in small pieces the polaroid of me as Chaucer and chuck it in the Thames, where, floating neither upstream nor down, it hangs on the turn of the tide.

Chaucer was unwilling to put the finishing touches to things or to reach conclusions. Four of his big works, including *The House of Fame* and *The Legend of Good Women*, he left incomplete. Judging by the plan for it, *The Canterbury Tales* is only a massive fragment. Was he indolent in his retirement or still too busy with public affairs? Did his mind tell him to keep slaving at the office and sod the poetry? My sense is that by rounding things off he knew that he was making it easier for his reader to escape what he meant.

Nobody knows what, except chance, gave him the idea for his masterpiece. But he started it in 1387, at least that short but massive 'Prologue', the account of each individual and every type who met at the Tabard on the way to Canterbury. One of those possible chances might be pure chance; we all know that our lives often depend on an instant. Another of the chances is that he took the trip himself that April when Philippa was ill, for she appeared to have died a month or two later; it would account for his view in the eighteenth line of the 'Prologue' that, if visited in the holy bliss of his absence, Becket had the people's power to 'holpen, whan that they were seke'.

The act of pilgrimage would also say committally that he loved Philippa well beyond personal convenience. Yet nothing is provable. Chaucer's privacy is under wraps for good. Not a single fact will ever be discovered or assumed to his discredit. Such deep anonymity is devoutly to be envied. But I have to believe he made the pilgrimage because I have to make a similar one myself. Any good journey is very slightly beyond imagination until you realise it in fact.

I began to think of all this as yet another way of writers, or anyone else for that matter (we are all the same at heart), never quite finding what they are looking for – the secret that edges away from you while you know it to be there. Relationships were like it, only good because you never quite got to the end of them; you never foresee how they can enrich you even as they slip away.

On a dun morning that threatens rain I take the 10.06 a.m. from Waterloo East to Canterbury West. I have photocopied, with map, the relevant pages in Michelin of the English capital of Christianity. The wheels grind slowly across the complex points above the Tabard, Borough Market, the tomb of Gower. Suburbs soon smear the window. The spirits soar. Here is a pilgrimage that lasts not four days but ninety minutes, if the train is on time. To Caunterbury we wende.

A first glimpse of Bell Harry, the immense tower of the cathedral, is caught between old warehouses adapted for use as discos, all picture-postcard, theme pubs dowsed in quaintness. Nothing is any longer quite right. But here and then, beneath the defensive bulwark of the Westgate, the pilgrims surged into town, the Stour river a moat under the arch. This one gate the pilgrims entered by is wide enough for four to walk abreast below the portcullis, a point now proved by a double-decker bus, wary of its wing mirrors, at walking pace. It passes through with respect.

Inside the city the scale further drops. St Peter's Street is made for midgets, the High Street, whichever is the smaller, for dwarfs. Even the sky makes me fear banging my head on it. Both streets, despite a lawless van driving with sloth, are now for pedestrians. They advertise leisure as a virtue. People are walking along them casually as if they owned their own space. To an ear used to cities it sounds like silence.

The ankle after that long plod from London is nearing its sacred goal. Here in the High Street I come upon exactly what a tired pilgrim wants. The St Thomas Hospital was founded soon after the martyr's life was rudely interrupted, to provide food and lodging for one night only for those too poor to stay elsewhere. At first glance the place not only headlines the past but reports it in detail. I hurry by with a resolve to return. For the moment I am aimed at other prey, a deconsecrated church called 'The Canterbury Tales'.

A queue stands outside it as for confession. Attendance is regimented. I ask which afternoon hour is best to try. Avoid three o'clock, says a voice behind the box-office glass that looks bulletproof, just where in this church of old the poor box would be found locked. Time is running short; I have to rattle out of this yesterday into the London present by early evening. That gives me an hour for a quick plunge into the St Thomas Hospital on the way to a quicker lunch.

But the moment I enter I am lost – as is time: here stands the fourteenth century in, for once, a literal guise. The only advice given, by the solemn man in charge, is that in those days hospital referred more to hospitality than illness; only later do I discover that pilgrims who were sick could stay more than one night. Otherwise I am left to pick up the past for myself, helped by an illustrated leaflet in French, for they have run out of the English version. With a shiver I think of Froissart passing in the street on one of his many English landfalls and fancying the *plie et frites* on a local chippy's blackboard; Canterbury takes euros as readily as groats.

The hospice speaks for itself. In the spaces bits of furniture, a long table, a jug of flowers, are suggestive of presences fevered by faith or hope or fear. There is a silence in the air open and musty enough to let in eras long gone. A tiny chantry lies under a low vault, built in 1375 for saying masses to the dead, which Chaucer might have seen only as a building site; in that year he was granted two wardships with due emolument in Kent. Below in the older undercroft the pilgrims, twelve at a time, slept their short nights. Above in a refectory they ate at fourpence a day under a garish mural of Christ, of which pastel scraps remain, the tints fading into an impression of mysticism, the details thrust into salience by being so few.

But it is the wooden roof of the chapel that captures me. Oak beams engage in a pattern of joinery that looks, to eyes blinking upwards from a cricked neck, like an abstract, a criss-cross of rising crucifixes, each worm-eaten chunk of wood nailed at all angles into the next, the pure structure lifting to the roofline. It feels like looking up through the layers at someone else's idea of God, an idea so simple as to void you of all complications.

Time is shortening. A Café Rouge offers the high-street simulacrum of a French lunch. I order a cross-Channel mussels and chips and a half-litre pitcher of white wine. In a minute I am

raising a glass to Froissart. In fifteen minutes no food has come.
An unhurried woman in the window gets mussels. It turns out
the waitress has dropped my helping. I see black shells skidding
across floors. Patience and humour, as in Chaucer, are the key to
existence. What do I know of Froissart? As a good reporter he
would probably ignore the incident rather than turn it into a
scandal. I dash out, fearing I will miss the fun, to visit 'The
Canterbury Tales'.

A line of French children has formed at St Margaret's Church.
They are vociferous. None is older than my teenage children,
except the mistress – a trim lady with irony in her bespectacled
eye. In the vestry, where closed doors advertise the entry to the
Tabard Inn, we are equipped with handsets, plus earphones that
offer commentary in a choice of languages. You are shown how
to hold the handset, when within, to avoid interference. It feels
in the hand like a time machine. All this palaver becomes a
passport to the fourteenth century.

By electronic means I am to be conveyed into an illusion that
might bring me closer to Chaucer than any effort of unaided
imagination. This is itself a facer: a short cut almost as radical as
watching the crucifixion broadcast live on the late news. I can
bypass the text of *The Canterbury Tales* by spending forty-five
minutes beyond that shut door with this bouncy cross-section of
Froissart's compatriots, relishing my own countryman's wisdom
and wit within the nutshell of this refashioned but antique
church, or I can quit.

The beer-bellied man handing out handsets has execrable
French which he enjoys using. The girls shout back asides in an
argot or accent he cannot catch. Between them the talk lands
slap in the midst of Middle English, half the words French, some

Latin, lots Anglo-Saxon; Chaucer meets Froissart in a big babble of words blurred by laughter.

And then the doors open.

Bizarrely I pass from a box office into the gloom of that inn in Southwark centuries ago. I see the spotlights. I detect the tricks. The actor's voice reverberates in my ear. I look at the waxwork figures, contorted into caricature, of pilgrims draped in sloshed slumber over the tables above which hams hang. The Host is telling us of the night's excesses, to be more than matched by his plans for tomorrow. I stare at a pale maid asleep amid the detritus of the feast, a figure who seems to echo Philippa Chaucer in her raunchy youth, and tiptoe past, really thinking I might wake her up if I put a foot wrong.

First the Knight's Tale, all romance, the characters picked one by one out of the darkness as the saintly chivalry of the story unfolds in the earphone. Three gothic windows of the actual church are suddenly suffused with stained-glass light. The Miller comes next, a voice known from television putting it over in rough Yorkshire. The graphic effect of Alison's shoving her bottom out of the window to receive a kiss from the unsuspecting Absalon, who then in revenge sears Nicholas's arse with a red-hot iron, is well timed. Your gut contorts in ribald response.

Is all this happening in your imagination? With its secret stairways and rooms of varying size at different levels, the church indeed feels like climbing about inside your own brain. It reduces you to childhood. Round the next corner there is sure to be something even more exciting to jump out at you – yes, the Wife of Bath and much curmudgeonly humour at the expense of sex and men, moving through to the Pardoner's dark account of three drunks hunting out death with intent to kill him. The whole display is a great big con that hurts and pricks your tears and laughs at you.

Meanwhile, as each episode darkens, another door slips open. Stretches of the Pilgrim's Way are glimpsed. Bushes I feel to be local brush the face. I gaze into thickets as Chantecler outwits the fox and see my own corner of Kent. As literally as yesterday, I walk into Borough High Street, naively looking out for landmarks. Every time I ease through another door into a new narrative, it is with an exquisite sense of having lost what I have just left. In advance I keep fearing what I might miss. I am also landed with the puzzling conceit that I have made it up myself.

The final tableau is the shrine to the martyr. Alongside the tomb of the Black Prince stands the altar surmounted with the casket containing St Thomas's remains which Henry VIII threw out. It is of solemn vulgarity, so almost jerks another tear. It also brings you back with a bump to what you have to regard as reality: the shrine of now, only yards away, in the cathedral.

Out in the air I hasten to the true chancel. There the Black Prince, buried on his back in 1376, still watches in effigy the desecration of Becket's shrine in 1538; his nose protrudes from his armour, thousands of hands have touched him for comfort or in prayer; this warrior has upstaged Becket by occupying the best seat in the house, the royal box. Nowadays only a fat candle burns on the site of Becket's old shrine.

The place where Becket in fact crumpled to his death, in a transept, is marked by a soppy plaque which, in lettering so trendy as to look already outmoded, records that Pope John Paul

II and Archbishop Runcie prayed by it side by side in 1982. Over this tablet in the floor hangs a violent sculpture that shows the swords jaggedly about to plunge into the martyr from on high – yet more out-of-date modernity – pointing down at the word 'Thomas', chiselled in oxblood italic into the paving below, a Becket sacrificed to typography, now a designer saint. It is less like honouring holiness than ogling an execution.

I hurry towards the station with plenty of time. There is a shop living off Chaucer. I nip in and buy seven reproductions of characters illustrated in the Ellesmere manuscript – cook, merchant, franklin, plus four clerics – throwing into the plastic bag Trevor Eaton's recording on tape of the Prologue in the authentic accent that sounds like a yokel off his rocker. At a glance the reading room of the public library is lined with men bent over a range of newspapers that are free as well as frightening to read. I feel the simple satisfaction of having been to 1382 and come back alive.

On the platform at Canterbury East I know there is further to go. I also know that if I persist in supposing that to whizz back and forwards in time is anything but illusion, I am deluded. Unless I think it is good for its own sake? I do. With any luck I have done less good to my ankle than to my brain.

Back at London Bridge in the half-dark, I toy with the discipline of walking back to Kennington via the Tabard. Sense wins. With an *Evening Standard* I wait in the cold for the driver of a 344 bus to bestir his limbs to the extent of flicking a fag out of the window and opening the doors. There has been a multiple rape in a suburb. Trains other than mine are still not running to time. A Cabinet minister defends a record that is described as indefensible. My hands are so chilled I can hardly turn the page.

Suddenly the engine chunters and roars. Soon we are dieseling down Borough High Street on the way home. By the front seat upstairs on a bus otherwise empty there is a banana skin underfoot.

II APRIL IN THE AEGEAN

A day later I am on the point of booking a car ferry from Dover to take a first look at Froissart's territory. But my wife springs a surprise. Wanting to celebrate a landmark birthday, she is treating the four of us to a cruise in Greek waters. While overjoyed by this interruption, I suspect there are things more dutiful to do than explore the eastern Mediterranean. I am, as it turns out, even more wrong than usual.

All right, the tedium: the sweat to the airport en route for Cyprus, hours of cramped knees, the cracks of aerial fear plastered over with drink, then the prospect of unknown people being unavoidable aboard the ship; the inescapability of being at sea, being inescapably middle-class at sea, being at sea with one's unavoidable self. Out from Larnaca, having settled into a nice cabin, I climb to a deck which happens to be deserted and, parallel with the ship, a hundred yards south of it, steadily flies a bird.

So unlikely is the presence of this one bird that I recognise it without putting a name to it, yet it is not to be mistaken: the long tail feathers, the deep beat of the wings, yes, a cuckoo. A kukkow, said Chaucer.

A cuckoo has set course for Syria. It has the loneliness of an explorer who knows where he is going, a rakish deceiver of a bird, a pirate ready for risk. For all the ship's power, the cuckoo is gaining on us, and I feel just a throb of that primordial pulse of fellow-feeling that like it or not binds me to all creatures that manage without machine or modernity. Soon the cuckoo is out of sight, and I ache for the fourteenth century, because that is where I am minded to be.

Then below decks, in our luxury cell, I realise the course we have set: I am on a crusade. The Crusades all came this way. Tomorrow's schedule allows for a visit to Saladin's castle in Syria or, as Chaucer calls it, Surrie; the knight would have known it or a lot about it; Chaucer's mind was furnished with detail of the Crusades, to him as sharp as such recent history as the Boer War. I am tuning into something just beyond my fingertips – five-finger exercises that will suddenly take off into a sonata, a phrase, a hint will set me going, they call it inspiration, I grit my teeth to snap it up, I stand stock still in the cabin in case it runs away from me, I carry it with care up a gangway that feels like a gangplank, and all through lunch, moving east towards the idea, I try to argue it into existence or close my mind so that the idea will take me by storm. But I go to have a nap disappointed and then, a seeming second later in the half dusk, I look out and there is Latakia, the harbour slowly engulfing this ship of mine, and it is then I realise I am sailing into the dark of Chaucer's mind.

If our Syrian hosts for this brief sortie into their land were no longer Saracens, we were certainly infidels, heavily armed with money and decked out in prejudice as stiff as armour. Everyone in Chaucer's time still bore the burden of those eight crusades between 1096 and 1271 which gave war a bad name and religion a worse one. They are a sorry record of a misplaced humanity poisoned by a love of Jesus.

The first crusade captured Jerusalem, which a century later Saladin won back during the second crusade, the third rewon territory but not Jerusalem, the fourth got diverted from its high purpose into the sack of Constantinople, the fifth fizzled out in Egypt, the sixth in 1228 clawed back Jerusalem only to lose it to the Turks fifteen years later, the seventh again foundered in Egypt, while the eighth lost heart when the King of France died on the way out. Whereafter Muslims kept their grip on the Holy Land until Israel popped up after the Holocaust.

The only known virtue practised by crusaders was chivalry (though not often to the opponent), which ideal of human conduct, especially as applied to the agonisingly slow seduction of beauteous virgins, had become a moribund formality by the time of the Hundred Years War. However, it remained the stuff of poetry to the romantic early days of Chaucer, Froissart and Boccaccio. Only when they thought twice, and caught a whiff of the prevailing wind, did they sit down, unpuzzled at last, and start to write revolutionarily.

As for Saladin (or Salah al-Din al-Ayyubi, 1137–93), he was born in the same city on the Tigris as Saddam Hussein and believed in jihad to his dying breath. Chivalry hardly came into the equation, or rather the total lack of one.

Somebody once told me that Francis Bacon, two centuries after Chaucer, was the last figure in history who had the capacity to contain all knowledge then open to man. So similarly had Chaucer, though less was at his disposal. But he knew all about conflicts in Syria between West and East. And this very sea under me was the basin of his education; Homer arose hereabouts in his mind, the gods fought over Troy in his boyhood games, the Greek myths seeped westward to the youth of Britain, the Bible in whatever guise walked down every London street.

The boy Geoffrey had no doubt picked up the bulk of it all in Southampton, legends from afar wafting inland from the quays, a culture picked up by osmosis from the sailors in the taverns, and just plain hard schooling. All you needed know of abroad was available at home. By the time he was past twenty his brain was idly packed with the sum of world scholarship. No one could take more on board. The rest was to be his invention.

We queue for a boat to the quayside, we crowd into a bus, we bowl up poor streets strung with laundry, we are in country shaggy with scrub, we stare at a sky where predators hang, we are as avid as a vulture for scraps of past, we are picking history apart, and I find I am looking back with envy at the ship, lolling there at anchor, knowing it all, full of experience, but at rest. The fancy takes me that the way the vessel is constructed, this well-named *Minerva*, resembles a simple model of the human brain.

Whose brain is it? It is Chaucer's brain. It is not until we return tired from touring the precipitous ups and downs of Saladin's castle and with relief are ferried back to Chaucer's brain that I realise how right I was.

I enter him as I set foot on board. I drag my ankle up a stairway to order a stiff measure of Geoffrey's daily intake. His unconscious is buried down among the engines. If I listen hard I hear it rumbling in harmony with the waves that break against the hull. I walk up and down the passages of his memory, the decks of cabins that all look the same but are uncommonly different: cells containing lives strange to me. As for me, I cast myself as a character wandering about Chaucer's mind, some virus from the future that has entered his imagination as he assembles, on this tour ranging widely in time and space in the lap of the Mediterranean, not only his education, but his future material. Yet consciously Chaucer knows as little of the interior workings of his own mind as I do of the immense mystery of the way this ship functions.

A vague absence takes a couple of days to identify. When you turn on the television in the cabin all you receive is someone you have just seen at lunch or who took your arm to steady you on a tour through this morning's ruins. So this is not a programme piped in from the outer world, but a scholar, also a passenger, talking about cult centres in the Aegean. By hobbling up to the lounge I can watch him giving the lecture in person. He too belongs to Chaucer's brain. So do his auditors, whether in cabin or lounge: we are all cut off from events elsewhere, we make our own, we are having none of the modern world reported to us, nor is anyone outside aware of what is happening within.

A cosy relief steals over me. I have been set at large in a smaller sphere. All it contains is the ancient world, and this floating time machine of ours is borrowed from Chaucer, crewed by Filipinos, cabin-staffed by Ukrainians, and commanded by British officers who will retire to Southampton's hinterland. That is, if our own world is still there when we sail back into it.

So, yes, the relief; the sea swims balmily past my window. In its waves there is no royal death or scandal. Spin doctors are not stirring it up. Because the wine-dark seas cannot be computed in terms of obvious value, there are no disagreements with the Treasury as to priorities. Health, education and transport are all in my hands; I am neither ill nor ignorant and I am on my way.

Today off the Turkish coast, on seas into which Icarus fell, we cruise past the Lycian tombs cut into the sheer cliff above Fetiye. Landing at Xanthus, I gaze in consternation at the huge stone covered on four sides with the as yet undeciphered Lycian, half Greek as on a blackboard, half cabalistic symbol with distances between capital letters as if the language were itself learning to read. In this city Brutus, unaware he was up against an enemy apt to commit suicide rather than lose, openly wept when he won. I long to understand the Lycians, as I do the Crusades, and all courage, folly, passion. As with the cuckoo on the voyage to Chaucer's Surrie, I am released into a mindset not my own.

Yet still a touch of the common in me yearns to go home. Off guard my finger stretches to the switch on the set in the cabin, forgetting there will be nothing but a lecture or a self-regarding image of the *Minerva* manoeuvring into harbour. In Antalya, wandering the streets where the passengers have been put out to shop, I spy a splash of English on a newspaper headline. It is a flimsy Turkish effort of four pages for tourists, but I am drawn to the vendor's hand that holds it; I desire it more than sugared sweetmeats or saffron that's a snip. I extend half a million lire, snatch the news from his greased palm, and sink to a stony seat by a fountain to read, to swallow the lies, to quench my thirst for stories, to learn what is happening in the paradise I have left behind at home.

But it's not like that. The limp rag curls its lip in my hands. The pages are boxed with ads that wink and leer. Night-clubs are the lure, round the corner here in Antalya, the belly-dancing eateries, the palaces of raki down that alley or this, sandwiched between scant news of elsewhere – the threat to the West of an Eastern stance that has Russian approval, a Scottish boy generously freed for a drug offence from the honour of staying in a Turkish prison. The real news, if anywhere, is in the small print.

Within a day or two we are off Delos. I see in this island dedicated to Apollo, as Chaucer's mind might, a sacred heart of the ancient world. At the jetty we climb off the lighter into legend. Nobody was allowed to be born or die here; nobody lives on it nowadays. Aeneas walks the streets on his path to Rome. Gods are everywhere but nowhere. The isle is pure past, all ruin. Time is waived. The pilgrims from the ship disperse across the confines of the island with no chance of refreshment without the foresight of hip flasks or a surreptitious roll buttered at breakfast. If we miss the boat back, we will be here all night.

Under a cold scud of cloud Chaucer's inner world is in chaos. The gods are angered. Fluted columns rise and fall in half-devastated ranks expecting to be grandly identified as temples. What were once houses cascade in marble niagaras down slopes that lead the eye up to summits that point at a watery eternity of sky. The logical footfalls of philosophers trod the now broken mosaic of the path close to the three-storey House of Hermes. Drinks were spilt on these mosaics, domestic quarrels stamped into them, slaves ran for their lives across them, tears wet them. Today the place is a lesson in the brevity of the imperishable.

I pick up a remnant or two of mosaic, hardly cohering, a quarter of a chessboard in less than miniature, and pop them into my pocket. Against the law I own half a dozen tiny cubes of history that don't fit together. Chaucer, barefoot or in sandals, was only a very few centuries closer to the artist or artisan who made this pattern for walking on. I finger my theft. I have stolen civilisation and intend to take it home in order to redefine it and I shall drink ouzo at the airport so as not to look guilty at customs. One day, having shared with my image of Chaucer whatever insight they offer, I shall return these marbles to Greece.

Theft? Just as I am stealing literally from a culture not my own, Chaucer stole from such foreign writers as Boccaccio, and written language was stolen – secretly, we will never know by whom – from the Mycenaeans: what does this tell me about cultural delinquency, building one's fortune and health at the expense of someone else, as a guest of the dead and gone?

It says that we have to be thieves to live and move on, a view less and less tenable as one afternoon we sail alongside Mount Athos. Here still functioning on this peninsula exclusive to males are the monasteries that were within Chaucer's range of knowledge. The attraction is to be alone in silence with only thought to entertain. Yet think of the blunting tedium of the sixteen-hour services, with never a sniff of the alcohol of the faithless life beyond; imagine, without a breath of fresh air, the continuously enforced return to prayer at set intervals. It is meant to be paradise on earth.

Here on board Holy Communion is served as the seas roughen. The concert room or lounge is converted without any problem into a temporary chapel. A touching address tells us that God is the person just closing the door behind Him when we enter the room, who turns the corner out of sight at the end of the street. The rising seas round Mount Athos are making the band's cymbals clash, the piano emits a twang, and we are told to keep our seats during the Gospel thanks to the stormy conditions the gods have brought to the Aegean.

The stately movement of the ship between islands – Rhodes, Samos, Lesbos, with landmarks near or far to port or starboard, as clear as light or shrouded in mist – is close to what thought is like. An hour's stop at Chios brings Homer out of the shadows. The whole of Rupert Brooke is caught in passing as an island recedes into the dusk. Sappho fades beyond the skyline. This voyage is capturing the nature of thought, its forward push, the rhythm of thinking things out, tending by compass rather than by eye to some destination too far to discern, widening the horizons narrowed by living a landlocked life, yet moving towards a mainland, Troy to the east, then westwards to Athens: this is the benison of this cruise in the moving vessel of Chaucer's mind. In these seas Troilus's impossible love for Cressida is making the heart give, even as I feel the pulse of the poet writing down the romance.

At intervals I enter the ship's library, the core of the brain, where I plunder Chaucer's culture and ignore all evidence of what has matured since.

Meanwhile a visceral obsession with being Chaucer, or being inside him, leads to the threshold of grotesque accidents on board. I draw back just in time from glancing on tiptoe into other people's cabins as if they were brain cells. I peer into the above-mentioned scholar's eyes as if expecting a magic wand will transform him into a clerk of Oxenford; he's a professor at Cambridge. In the bar I hover over tables occupied by substantial women, looking for a Wife of Bath to play into my hands. The cleric who took the service might at a pinch make one of the nun's priests. On the ship I sense that all these characters are forming in Chaucer's mind – this journey is occurring before *The Canterbury Tales* but after he has got *Troilus and Cressida* under his belt. I simply know this, or do I merely choose it as my moment? I, and I'm not alone, always want to be an actor and hide behind a part, to reveal me to my own shocked eyes, if not on a public stage. The life so short, Chaucer tells me, the craft so long to learn.

This morning, sea legs tottering on to land, we spend at Mycenae where writing got lost for two centuries. In a decrepit bus we pass 9,000 years at speed gazing up at Argos, the oldest city continuously inhabited in Greece. A Frankish castle of 1204 tops the hill which by whatever form of signal sent Clytemnestra the message that sealed Agamemnon's doom in his bath. Back at sea the chest involuntarily sobs. Tears run. It is all too much, not to take in, but to credit. I am a lost civilisation, a written language that hiccuped into silence, a passenger on a cruise, a man of the media, a devotee of lunch, not to mention being myself, while cuckooing into Chaucer's psyche.

Tomorrow we will be sailing into Athens, where Chaucer set *The Knight's Tale*, having borrowed the plot from Boccaccio, and then flying home to Kent via Gatwick.

III SPRING IN KENT

To prepare for an invasion of France on a date undecided, I drive down to Kent on a spring evening. At a red light, I pass the spot where Chaucer's pilgrimage paused for refreshment at St Thomas a Waterings, 2 miles out from the Tabard. A vendor tries to sell me the *Evening Standard* through the window, but I want no news.

Here stood Surrey's equivalent of Tyburn for hanging villains, now interred (I like to think) under the Tesco in the Old Kent Road. Here the Host determines by lottery who of the party shall tell the first tale. Every schoolboy failing an exam knows the 'verray parfit gentil knight' from the 'Prologue' to *The Canterbury Tales*, a figure of the utmost honour who in far-flung parts fights to preserve civilisation as he knows it, chivalry personified, but no cipher, a chap of flesh and blood. When he drew the short straw for the first story he gave in with grace and for material betook himself to Athens which I have just left. The light turns green.

The last of the rush hour peters out in Lewisham towards the M20. The blossom in suburban streets darkens into luminosity, scent streaming in at the half-open window: all desirably familiar, this extension of the Old Kent Road. Pubs called

Thomas à Becket or Wife of Bath light up at intervals. I am
about to enter the black tunnel that leads at dead of night into
the secrets of the fourteenth century.

An electronic signboard indicates the M20 is closed between
Junctions 2 and 3. With the cockiness of a gambler convinced
that just this once he is bound to win I sail past the slip road at
Junction 1. Ahead of me stretches a nightmare city of glowing
reds as drivers pump their brakes. Hazard lights blink in rage. I
am in the fast lane at a standstill.

Up ahead it's some drunk, of course, who in an accident has
murdered time for thousands of us. He missed a juggernaut's
signal to pass and rammed his engine into its tailboard. He was
trying to outwit death. In a period of plague he was the fellow in
The Pardoner's Tale who a while ago had been hanging around
one of the pubs I saw receding in the rear mirror. Two chums
were with him, all well over, not only the top, but the limit.
Now the two less pissed are in the back and the one most drunk
is the driver, and in the plastered noise they create as they career
along the motorway towards home and hangover, they hear
nothing of what life is like except that you can kill death. Then
the smash happens.

In *The Pardoner's Tale* the three revellers who unsteadily set
out to put death to the sword are told by a passer-by that the
culprit is taking his ease under a certain tree up the road. Across
the central reservation I strain to see this tree in the dark. The
drunks make haste and behold, under one of those overpower-
ing Kentish trees that seem to shadow whole meadows, piles of
gold and silver heaped for the taking. The trio confers in joy.
This hoard can only be nicked by night. The youngest alcoholic
is sent back to the last exit to fetch more wine from the nearest

town, while the other two keep watch. Amicably they resolve to
kill him, so as to share between them the deadly goods that are
their future.

> This youngest, which that wente un-to the toun,
> Ful ofte in herte he rolleth up and doun
> The beautee of thise florins newe and brighte.
> 'O lord!' quod he, 'if so were that I mighte
> Have al this tresor to my-self allone,
> Ther is no man that liveth under the trone
> Of god, that sholde live so mery as I!'
> And atte laste the feend, our enemy
> Putte in his thought that he shold poyson beye.

The cars move slowly on in threes, while I await their friend's
evil return up the hard shoulder to the base of the tree of
treasure. With him, in his unsteady progress, he brings three
bottles of wine, the first as pure as the red for which my tongue
now longs, the other two topped up with poison strong enough
to wipe out survivors of the plague. But of course they all die in
this conspiracy of greed at the foot of the fruitful tree, where
Adam too perished of the more innocent sin of being seduced by
a woman of his own making.

The delay lasts six hours. Well after midnight I reach Junction
2 and, as luck rarely has it, I am the first car not to be deflected on
to the jammed minor roads but waved on down the motorway.
Triumph tenses my veins, my head bursts into inchoate song, I
drive at ninety to catch up time. Not a vehicle is visible ahead of
me. I have got a start on everyone. I am the first ever to explore
this triple-laned path that leads straight into the past, the first to

take this pilgrimage, the first to be getting a grip on the three heroes – now Chaucer, with two still to come – who parallel my present.

The dark house in Kent lights up at a touch. The rooms are chilled with disuse.

Spring has not quite infiltrated them. A spider stalks out of hiding across the kitchen floor. Last year's webs hang with corpses. A queen wasp lazily attacks a window from the inside. In a trap still baited with old cheese a mouse lies dead with a drop of blood on a bared tooth. Among the timbers of the roof jackdaws clack and gurgle. Going to bed, writhing into cold pyjamas, is racked by the shivers of joining a household occupied by forces as feral as disease.

A hidden army in the house hems me in. Stings or infections might at any moment sidle out of the woodwork. Lying in bed, waiting for a day taking too long to dawn, I reflect on age-old images, haunting our minds from the year dot, of the earth opening up and spewing forth a volcanic evil. Here the locals say that the field next door to this house, a rumpled grave of the old village, has never been excavated lest the plague escape from it, breathe into our homes, bulge our armpits and groins, cough black blood out of our mouths. To block it all out the foetal position is best, the sheet a shroud, the pillow an earplug.

In the spring of 1348 the Black Death sidled into Europe from an unknown source in the Orient as a result of trade. Mariners brought it first to Sicily where it more than decimated Messina. The angry city chased off the sailors, only to spread the disease throughout mainland Italy. Man blamed man for the undiagnosable, for the horror of the symptoms, for a disaster so comprehensive as to be beyond comprehension, for the almost instant death in agony of anyone close to you, wife, child, lover. The visuals and soundtrack of a struggling body were blinding, deafening, in their heartbreak as a beloved went out of life choking out blood and prayer and bacilli.

Here the bookshelves are dotted, in index or footnote, with news of the Black Death. The detail takes some finding; lots of books are still in the remover's cartons. We have only just settled into the fourteenth century in Kent. The first fact to emerge, as I kneel on the brick floor tearing sticky tape off the cardboard box containing the evidence, is that (doubtless) in 1348, at some time in early summer, the disease (possibly) landed in Southampton where the boy Chaucer (probably) was four. All is unpinnable down, history's nature to spin away from posterity.

Thus the source of the Black Death in England might well be Calais, where a siege was in progress or just over. A ship supplying Edward III's investing forces returned to its home port of Southampton with infection aboard, either in the form of black rats crawling with fleas or sailors already bitten. Medical science never focused on the scurry of rats. Fleas were too tiny to suspect. The vessel containing the unknowable tied up in a seaport that remained ignorant for centuries after a third of its people had died in agony. They thought it could come only from God.

If the spread was fast, the statistics were incredible. Within weeks the plague had entered every Channel port unseen. In Kent people to bear corpses to the grave were in as short supply as the space for graves or time to dig them in. A third of the garden of England was reported by a monkish eye in Rochester to be abandoned to nature. Chaucer's survival may have been purely due to the odd chance that the lowest incidence of death was in children aged from six to ten, 7 per cent compared to 46 per cent of those in their late fifties. Clerics, in particular that monk, were quick to pounce: vice had gripped the population, evil was rife, depravity had taken hold of youth, not to mention workers. Saving souls as a profession had surrendered its charms. One parish lost three vicars in two months and had to wait for a fourth.

France, where Jean Froissart was eleven, by no means escaped the slaughter of 1349, though Liège, not far from Valenciennes, and an area to the east of Calais were largely, inexplicably, spared the plague. In Normandy black flags flew on the churches. On her way to be sumptuously married in Spain a daughter of Edward III caught it in Bordeaux. Much liquor was looted by those too poor to join in any pointless exodus. It was better to die dead drunk after as much lechery as you could lay hands on, even if one French theory had it that sex vulnerably overheated the metabolism. It certainly did in Tournai, a stone's throw from Froissart's birthplace, where a chronicler recorded that 'dances, festivals, games and tournaments continued perpetually; the French danced, one might say, on the graves of their kinsmen'. Doctors were as little trusted for a cure as nowadays we trust priests for a message or newspapers for the facts. Nobody had any power over the plague. You had at best a week or two left, if not a day.

Not all was bad. In Florence, worst hit of Italian cities and almost twice as big as London, the Black Death gave Giovanni Boccaccio his best idea. He would gather a group of young people elegantly panicked by the disease preying on their streets and pack them off on horseback, as on a pilgrimage, into the hills above Florence, antiseptic with sweet scents floating on pure air, to challenge them – as the Host challenged the social muddle and mix who gathered in his inn to go to Canterbury – to tell stories that might take their minds off reality while tickling up their libidos and inducing in them some sort of a moral sense and allowing them (with the help of his genius) to invent the shorthand language of film in a series of sitcoms.

Boccaccio was to preface this *Decameron* with the most vivid account of the pestilence as it affected his home town ever penned, as though he were also claiming credit for inventing documentary. The plague lasted six months; more than 50,000 Florentines died. In his opening Boccaccio was the eyewitness out of heaven, every phrase a gobsmacker that made you feel sick with symptoms – of fear, anxiety, loss – slowly gathering in your spirit. He wrote with the adrenalin in his veins of having just beaten the odds.

Here in Kent our village was evacuated by the Black Death. The quietude of the hamlet where we live next door to its mighty church was assured for ever by an age-old decision to build a new village a mile away, as if a whole community had determined to shake that memory of sickness from its mind.

The mice have made nests out of our stock of lavatory paper. Outside the window bees are arabesquing in the air. At a clap of the hands the jackdaws depart in panic.

I turn on the *Today* programme on Radio 4. Someone has again strapped explosives to his belly and at a touch set ablaze a coachload of innocents with nuts and bolts hammering into their faces. Somewhere in Italy a fascist has topped the poll. A famine is in progress across an area of Africa forty times the size of Wales.

Nothing has changed since Chaucer reported versions of such things, except that the news has taken less than a year to reach me and is more than mere rumour. Hard facts are now instantaneous.

For days there has been no one about. Quivers of change occur in the body which you only notice when alone: corruption within, of each day drawing nearer death. The ankle deteriorates from both strain and disuse, the joints in the fingers seize up, a pain in the lower back might be muscular or lie deeper below the flesh in an incurable organ. Solitude believes there will be no time to fetch help before the things that plague me take a turn for the worse.

So, aching legs tucked into a blanket, I sit and watch the plague of television. A property developer is convicted of manslaughter after hiring two thugs to stab a businessman, a peer perverts the course of justice, a respected doctor has killed hundreds of patients, thousands of council workers strike over low pay, millions are lost on the stock markets. From the lectern the face of the newscaster is a steady gleam: each fact matters as little as the last or next. But the lure persists. A girl of eleven got her lip trapped while scanning an image of her face into a computer. Firemen freed her. Meanwhile in 1368 Chaucer is leaving the country in plenty of time to meet Froissart.

That evening at home in Kent the bells ring out behind the boom of the set. With difficulty I pick my way under the beams, banging my head but not enough to see stars, and wrench the back door open on the starry evening. The clangour is immense in a wind that shakes the lilacs. The ringers are just doing their regular practice, but the resonances propel clashes of victory or warning into the treetops. It is an old sound. Under the bells a vision of the archbishop's palace in the next field arises in the dusk.

While huge in the open air, the throb of bells sounds more intensely in the head. It carries an echo of the Borough on that headache of a morning when the pilgrims set off for Canterbury in a rout sharply disciplined by the Host. It sounds out across Romney Marsh to welcome ashore the errant vessel that in 1361 brought Jean Froissart first to England. And, as I machine back and forth in time with an access of elation, it is simultaneously the repeated knell and toll of Florence as Boccaccio hurries about his business during the plague, choosing the church of Santa Maria Novella to launch his chosen cast of beautiful people into the safety of the hills to escape death by telling stories.

The afternoon is migraine heavy; a siesta feels like the onset of sickness. The weather darkens. If thunder moves in, the lights will cut out. There are candles, but where? The phone rings inside the house while I am trying to concentrate on *The Knight's Tale*. My ankle fails to get vertical in time to catch the call. There is a garbled message about a pilgrimage. It seems a hoax. Here is a neighbour talking about a pilgrimage. I am surely being teased. Two local women have ridden their horses from the next-door village of Bonnington all the way to Santiago de Compostela in Spain. Why would they do a thing like that? It must have taken months.

Minutes later the parish magazine arrives in the letterbox, the only sound for hours to slither into the silence. I saw no one deliver it. In the village there is no priest either to bury a corpse or to edit a magazine, for we are between rectors, much as when Erasmus was nominally in charge of the village's spirit but never turned up to nourish it. The magazine records, as fact, tomorrow's celebration at St Rumwold's in Bonnington of the pilgrimage by the two women on horseback to Santiago de Compostela in Spain. To match their spirit I shall walk to the church. If I start now, with a stick, on a crutch – no, it's three miles. I look at the car.

All by itself at Bonnington this bulge of a church squats on the edge of the Marsh: St Rumwold, a saint so holy he only lived a day. However much I strain the senses, the scene is deserted, the silence seemingly seamless. As usual when you leave off your watch, I have a sharpened sense of exact time, mildly irritating. The two women plus consorts and cohorts must by now have left the village and be winding down the lane.

Behind distant trees a glint of metal is on the move: slow, not a car, and then that clop of hooves, a percussive counterpoint on the tarmac, and into view, round a curve, ride the two women at a walk, escorted by two knights on foot in chainmail, helmets noble, visors aflash in the sun; and behind them pages or squires dressed in that androgynous blend of skirts, stockings, doublets, that looks stagey until, unwitnessed by others, you see it unfolding on a country lane across the vast flat of Romney Marsh. In the procession girls follow with long dresses flowing from their hips.

A local couple, whom I met only last week at someone's dinner party, carry off a flourish of anachronism in their garb, looking as vivid as jesters. But the spirit in this suddenly populated waste of the Marsh is not of a pageant but a pilgrimage. Nobody is prancing or acting, they are living themselves; above all, not regressing, not patronising the past for the present's sake. Thus it was, thus it looked, on a lonely extreme of the Pilgrim's Way for hundreds of years, threatened by such evils as plague, famine, banditry, but at least unfettered by the media, unless you count Chaucer or the parish magazine.

With a slowness agonising to modern impatience the Middle Ages process into the church. The two pilgrims in skin-tight riding breeches stand under the pulpit. A mixture of times weaves in and out of the celebration in words and music. From Walter Raleigh comes 'the scallop-shell of quiet' (many present are wearing shells safety-pinned to the breast) inspiring our hope. The handsome fellow in doublet and hose who will soon barbecue frankfurters looks to be Raleigh's current incarnation. From Bunyan comes 'He who would valiant be', arousing our courage with one or two heart-rending errors on the organ, while a priest austere in black cassock stands drably in for that puritan. Out of the mists and mysticism of the fourteenth century Walter Hilton, printed on the order of service, presses on us the pilgrimage of the spirit that will lead to the unleashing of our love, and in seconds tears blur the candles in the slant of afternoon light, a child runs at random up the aisle, the chest painfully expands to manage the excess of feeling, and everybody is hugely at one.

Everybody is at one. The priest then – on a pilgrimage, he murmurs, 'The church walks with humanity' – steps in as anchor man to question the two bonny adventuresses on their motives. The first says she wanted to do something difficult before she was too old. Her sister wanted simply to undertake as long as possible a ride for charity. This is sincerity under the spotlight; we are almost watching television. Here is a priest conducting his service as a chat show. We in this happy congregation take in the narrative of the pilgrimage not in the sweeps that might once have done it justice, but in gulps to suit today's appetite. Fast food is already smoking into the church from the barbecue by the tombstones.

We have just been told a story.

Once this media moment is over, commercials enter in the form of prayers. Meanwhile, all three church doors wide open to the thrill of the afternoon, the horses are cropping grass off the graves that still push up daisies, and the scent of meat grilling wafts into the church, adding a new yearning to the deeper ones already satisfied. We all dash out and eat with a will, leaning on tombs, unwrapping teas of cling-filmed sandwiches and cakes, feeling rocky in the sunshine, pouring down non-alcoholic drinks as hued as tropical fruit. Erasmus, who would have liked it in these parts, had he followed up his appointment as rector of Aldington in the late 1400s, once followed in Chaucer's footsteps on pilgrimage to Canterbury.

Fire smoking, doors open, people chatting, friends in the making, the churchyard is just the place for the Host (where is he?) to call for a story from whomsoever (squire, sailor, lawyer, merchant, clerk?) is next on his eccentric roster. We have paused for refreshment on our pilgrimage at St Thomas a Waterings. We need a diet more rich than backchat: the roughage of narrative, the protein of a plot, the stringy texture of character, the real meat of life. The Knight gets the job.

A glance round the church assures me I can cast the story to the full. Waiting to enter, the knight who escorted the twin stars on horseback still has his helmet on. Others are wearing the right outfits. The nave is packed with extras in patched sackcloth. I think back to the beginnings of the painful plot of *The Knight's Tale*. In an appalling threesome, Palamon and Arcita are two best friends stricken at first sight by the same heart-stopping girl called

Emily. When they glimpse her from the tower of a prison in Athens, their undying devotion to each other comes almost to blows. For Palamon she exists only through the bars of his cell; his love feeds on being a helpless voyeur with nothing to occupy his mind. By then Arcita has been exiled; for him Emily exists, but no less strongly, in the imagination, which injects him with doses of lethal romance.

To cut a long story short (which form of words the Knight keeps using to make sure of not losing his grip on his pilgrim audience), this opening of the tale is a heady climax to the idea of courtly love. It also sets in motion a cliffhanger teeming with ideas, places, conventions new to me: another world to live in, an invitation to alter my mental ways. A chance to change.

But wait, I have just had one. I put the Knight on hold, to stick to the story here and now: two women, determined to be faithful to the pilgrimage's original path to Santiago, trotting through underpasses in Paris against every by-law, the speed of the autoroute lorries blasting the horses aside under a fast-train viaduct roaring overhead, their spirits upheld by the innumerable and nameless others who had wended this way before them over the centuries, until they eventually come out into the relief of open country and our heroines are back on the trek south. If that wasn't a story, what is?

We have been granted a modest version of the tale just now in church, bitten back, mostly withheld, told with wry grimaces, underplayed for all it is worth. But we have listened entranced, the sun in our eyes.

The next morning, without haste but with speed, I proceed to Dover, not on horseback or on foot, but at the wheel of the Renault Clio. In July 1368 Chaucer was granted a passport from

Dover, thus making him too late to join the party for his patron Prince Lionel's second wedding in Milan that May, unless it was a bash lasting all of three months. But was he perhaps on some secret mission for the King? Certainly, two years later, he was given letters of protection from Edward III when abroad on the King's service from June to Michaelmas. Driving one-handed, I pat my passport in my pocket for comfort. Next to it is a folded photocopy of *The Knight's Tale* for easy reference to a sphere that can unlock my mind from its habits. I also have my complete Chaucer with me, seven volumes in the boot, an 1895 Froissart in the Lord Berners translation, and a Penguin Boccaccio for reading in bed.

The heart sings. There is no queue on the M20, no tailback, no despair. Communications are restored. We are on the move.

IV SUMMER IN FRANCE

From the downs that used to carry the southern lap of the Canterbury pilgrimage, I descend towards Dover. The world's busiest shipping lane hoves into view. My hands tighten on the wheel with an excitement only just not infantile.

All life hangs before me and below me and beyond me. In the far haze a few ships are just visible, a tanker or two in outline, a fishing boat closer inshore, a suspicion on the horizon that might be a smudge of France.

I am not listening to news on the radio. Nor is there a cross-Channel ferry in sight. I drive on down, with every hope of launching a pilgrimage into Froissart's France just across the way. The mind shimmies back to the very first Canterbury tale told at Tesco on the site of St Thomas a Waterings in the Old Kent Road, when the Knight marched off into the Europe of the classics for his story. I think too of that other grand surprise: the party at St Rumwold's celebrating the two women who rode to Santiago, when I half expected an attendant knight to break into a tale of chivalry and courtly love. A ghost of both, classical Athens, medieval Spain, was implicit in the quiet English manners that rose to each occasion. Meanwhile the brain is crowded with the excitement of going abroad: to unmask Jean Froissart, that sycophant of royalty.

I draw into the ferry terminal. Not only must I pay £10 extra for failing to book a passage in advance, but a strike has shut down contact with France all morning. There is no news as yet. The best Dover can boast on the harbour front is a hotel once august. Its social areas have been done up all plush and trashy. The beer sinks as heavily as the sandwich. Here I am, stuck, brain racing, not a thought in my head, glimpsing but not crossing the sea. I toy with alternative plans. I can roar north and cover Froissart's visit to Scotland. Or his visit of homage to Richard II at Windsor? Perhaps, but no; I drive back to the terminal.

And the strike is over. All of a sudden I am steering with hilarity into the multiple-lane queue for the first P&O ferry to loom out of the stoppage.

Ignoring the ankle, I begin a spritely climb up deck after deck to the heights of the ship. Only the top of the world is good enough. My head reels from the fumes of oil. Yet under the huge sky the prospect, and my prospects, look at once better than ever, full of ships going far and ships coming in, darkened by outlines of a continent where the past waits in ambush. I am a soldier going to the wars, a captain on the bridge weighing up the risks, a conqueror in the making, a writer with his heart in his mouth, and I go below into the miasma of fry-ups underlying the reek of boiled coffee, and nonetheless with appetite think of the depths under me and the heavens over me and the towers and cranes of Calais ahead.

Close the eyes for a minute, and swimmers from two centuries are breaking records as they pass the ferry, Blériot is flying unsteadily overhead below the wispy dogfights and the waves of Goering's bombers, the paddle-steamers are loaded to the gunwales with an exhausted army beached at Dunkirk, St

Augustine in a lonely boat bobs towards the foundation of Canterbury, and with a humour caught from Chaucer and an accuracy I look for in Froissart, I am already well into an hour of freedom from time, a pause as renewing as a night's sleep, as the troopships aimed at the Somme are crowding the Channel with fear disguised as fun, Henry in ideal weather has set his course to outshine his French counterpart on the Field of the Cloth of Gold, Caesar gives him a wide berth in galleys making for a land that will chill the hot blood of Romans for four centuries, and to the westward toss the Norman ships on their way to a beach near Hastings that will forever knit us to France, and it all happens to be happening at once in the one place that matters: me!

There in Henry VIII's reign at Calais – a skyline is emerging – the Froissart *Chronicles* were first put into English under grey clouds by Lord Berners. The city still belonged to England then, if only just, and Berners was appointed governor by Henry and commanded to translate. Mobile phones squeal or carol in the bar, voices pitched high enough to address a foreigner but only assuring home of their proximity to Calais. Women as raucous as seagulls discuss last night's episode of a soap while buoys clang outside. Men with pints stare at tabloid headlines too big to grasp. Any reference to *The Knight's Tale* is as far from me as any reality of Europe.

We land at Calais. Eyes glued to the wrong side of the road, I bump over cobbles on the way to the arena of public buildings lost in parks that seems to be the centre. An illusion, for the real old city is ringed by canals and basins and quays, patchwork streets lined with young buildings in this most often destroyed town of the last millennium – endlessly rebuilt on ruins, out of ruins. Half an eye is out for any seedy hotel that may have survived war upon war. I need a night here, feather-bedded, high-bolstered, to know how Lord Berners felt in the isolation of Calais when, as governor, he undertook for Henry both to strengthen the fortifications and to realise Froissart. It seems a way through to the chronicler.

I drive round inspecting my fiefdom as John Bourchier, Lord Berners, born 1467, all my ancestors in public service (one indeed fought at Crécy); educated at Balliol, years of travel abroad, became a soldier, grew into a king's favourite, made Chancellor of the Exchequer for life at forty-five; thank goodness for democracy. This paragon rides at ease through my part of Kent when attending Henry at the Field of the Cloth of Gold; the Privy Council rewards him with thanks for an account of that fabulous event – and then, suddenly, in Calais, lots of bright lights: a chain hotel on an inner ring road, which I earmark in case nothing better turns up.

I stop in a square where a decrepit church, Nôtre Dame, a legacy of enemy action now shut down as too dangerous to enter, propped up by awkward buttresses, contains his lordship's remains. Berners died in office in 1532 at sixty-five.

With a look at the menus outside a restaurant tipped by Michelin for good value, a glance within shows that, like Calais after the siege in 1346, it is heavily colonised by the English. These dowdy conquerors, waiting for a late ferry with their car boots full of booze, face one another in a perspective of tables like dummies in a window display.

Down street after street the cobbles narrow into vistas of parked cars, the shutters closed on the glimmer of television.

Only that ring-road hotel where I now check in has a faint air of being alive, if not lively.

In its dull oblong of dining room the simplicity in the menu suits a fancy for fare common to Chaucer and Froissart. They too ate here in Calais – maybe *potage, omelette, fromage,* who knows, if not the *frites* I risk ordering in an act of reckless anachronism; they too drank their *ordinaire* to the dregs. Nor do they miss the the mood of the music that throbs just below hearing, songs full of that French ache for love, going, going, gone, as in the lyrics of Guillaume Machaut, the composer who touched both their *oeuvres* with the self-indulgence of his melancholy.

From the bar, pool balls click. A news bulletin is mumbling on a hidden set. Most of the diners are solitary with newspapers propped up by carafes, thin men with short hair in glasses, men plumpening into middle age, a lone woman lost in a magazine: everyone being everyman being anonymous. In this public room, devoid of private talk, the media become ironically a defence against intrusion.

A table by the hatstand has a messy bevy of local papers limp from overuse. Hundreds of hands have wrinkled their pages since at dawn they rolled fresh off the presses. If still just in date, they are dead. The news is now newer. In my own brand of defence I slide from my pocket, next to the passport, the photocopy of *The Knight's Tale* and am at once transported into a basic sketch of what they are reading in their tiring newspapers: life. Life.

I am quickly into the action. In my mind's eye Chaucer strolls through Smithfield. With his clerkly mind he is gauging the likely effect of the tournament stands the King has commissioned him to plan and erect. Meanwhile the Knight on the road to Canterbury has drawn me to that jousting field in Athens where Palamon and Arcita are to fight out their love for Emily. On the background radio, the crackle of news now over, the cheers swell from some match in the French provinces.

The teams of knights supporting their heroes are trumpeted into battle. In no time blood gushes. The spears spur on. Swords flash silver, breastbones cave in, horses crash sideways. The verses pound vividly on and on, as hypnotic as the gallop, the shouts of shock, the thump of bodies encased in metal hitting the earth. The words shine new-forged off the page, yelwe outyellows the modern, col-blak outdoes coal black, dyamaunt is brighter than diamond, citryn sharper than lemony. Look anywhere, the very language is more savoury than the cheese I am finishing, a lot fuller than this last swill of wine. The cheers rise in volume. Someone has won. On the bloody floor of the restaurant, unobserved by faces lost in magazines or hidden behind broadsheets, kings are dying, knights in armour writhing under a weight of pain, horses in reflex kicking against fatal wounds. Tomorrow rump steak will be on the menu.

But abruptly, as I sit here, memory kicks in: Rodin's great image of the fourteenth century stands, centrepiece of a municipal park, in the heart of this town. In a sweat, embarrassed, I am forgetting the urgent, the visible, the now. In the paperback locked in the Clio boot in the car park, Froissart is telling the whole story, which Lord Berners is translating. After his Crécy win, Edward III laid siege to Calais for a year. He starved it out. The populace had run out of rats to eat by the time six rich burghers, stripped to shirt and breeches, halters round their necks, volunteered to hand over the keys of the walled city to the English king. I swallow the last of my cheese. I have a drama on my doorstep.

> Then the captain went with them to the gate [writes Jean Froissart according to Berners], there was great lamentation made of men, women and children at their departing: then the gate was opened and he issued out with the six burgesses and closed the gate again, so that they were between the gate and the barriers. Then he said to sir Gaultier of Manny: 'Sir, I deliver here to you as captain of Calais by the whole consent of all the people of the town these six burgesses, and I swear to you truly that they be and were today most honourable, rich and most notable burgesses of all the town of Calais. Wherefore, gentle knight, I require you pray the king to have mercy on them, that they die not.

Sir Walter Manny promises to do his best, but Edward III will not listen, 'for greatly he hated the people of Calais for the great damages and displeasures they had done him on the sea before'. As Froissart puts it, 'Adont se grigna li rois et dist: "Manni, Manni, soufrés vous. Il ne sera aultrement." Mesires Gautiers de Manni n'osa plus parler, car li rois dist moult ireusement: "One fache venir la cope teste! Chil de Calais on fait morir tant de mes hommes que il convient ceuls morir aussi."

'Adont fist la noble roine d'Engleterre grand humelité.' Or, as Berners phrases and pursues the passage:

> Then the king wryed away from him and commanded to send for the hangman and said: 'They of Calais have caused many of my men to be slain, wherefore these shall die in like wise.'

Then the queen, being great with child, kneeled down and sore weeping said: 'Ah, gentle sir, sith I passed the sea in great peril, I have desired nothing of you; therefore now I humbly require you in the honour of the Son of the Virgin Mary and for the love of me that ye will take mercy of these six burgesses.'

The king beheld the queen and stood still in a study a space, and then said: 'Ah, dame, I would ye had been as now in some other place; ye make such request to me than I cannot deny you.'

I reach Rodin in the summer dusk. The masterpiece stands alone on an expanse of sward at the front of a public building. The burghers are black in bronze, desperate in attitude, high strung with dignity, hoping for a life without assuming a right to it, heroes, fools, martyrs, tycoons, all involved in one tense mass, now art. They were the elite of Calais, ready to surrender their lives. Rodin knew in the gnarled contortion of his fingers what he was moulding: France, the spirit of France at her lowest ebb, when begging for mercy from a foe across the Channel, a France rising in dignity to answer to a humiliation, the France that rang in Froissart's heart when he tried to be fairminded in his views of the 100-year clash between the two countries – the very France at this minute crammed with English tourists, in the centre of whose London, in gardens below the Houses of Parliament, stands a replica of Rodin's Burghers of Calais; how closely, I shiver in thinking, we share a destiny. Yet nobody is around to notice any of it. Everyone is doing what I now go back to do.

In the box of my bedroom, the whole of Western Europe enters through a screen that apes the shape of the window,

which looks out on a town besieged by boredom. Neck cricked
on a bolster, I run at speed through nine channels. Several
variants on France nudge aside a few frames of Belgium which
give way to some faulty England, while Holland is fuzzy and
Germany almost non-existent. There is no Italy at all. Though in
Calais, gateway to Europe, I start feeling hollowed out by this
inner bankruptcy of channel-hopping, jamming scraps of next to
nothing into your brain too fast, amid gales of studio laughter.
My eyes doze over the mishmash and an hour later I awake to
the nightmare of a station that has not yet closed down and will
never stop playing games and giving prizes and making fools for
us and fools of us. I switch off. The window will not open.

In next morning's fresh air, a few miles out of Calais, the Field of
the Cloth of Gold must be worth a detour, if only because Lord
Berners as courtier accompanied the patron of his translation:
'Here begynneth', he began, 'the first volum of sir Johan
Froyssart: of the cronicles of Englande, Fraunce, Spayne, Por-
tyngale, Scotlande, Bretayne, Flanders, and other places adioy-
nynge. Translated out of Frenche into our maternal englysshe
tonge by Johan Bourchier, knight, lorde Berners: At the co-
maundement of oure moost highe redouted soverayne lorde
kyng Henry the viii., kynge of Englande and of Fraunce and
nigh defender of the christen faythe, etc.' The site lies off the
route to Crécy but on my inner itinerary, a royal occasion fixed
in my head as the dying gasp of chivalry, which was already
running out of puff in Froissart's time more than a century earlier
– though he forced on chivalry a final kiss of life by writing in
respectful terms of the European monarchs who still clung to its
manners.

But in June 1520 came positively the last appearance, this grand finale. Ranks of marquees with spiked turrets composed of fine-spun, gold-embroidered stuff dazzle the child's mind in me and always did, an infant's drawing with festoons of bunting dancing in primary colours; and the glare of the sun on gilded tunics ablaze with lions, to which an open-air Shakespeare production in Regent's Park bears a tawdry resemblance, and the poetry melts into the air like gold pouring from the lip of a crucible; and there in that very phrase is out-and-out romance for you in all its yuck. I see the flags racing in the wind atop tall gold poles as the two nations (to this minute in the amity of enmity) make yet another show of sealing an eternal friendship that never lasts.

The commemorative stone is easy to miss. It stands at the roadside, almost in the ditch, only twice as big as those stones also in Picardy, which in relentless ranks record the deaths of soldiers of the Great War known only to God, but not like them in ranks, white, white, white: this one alone, singular, as granity grey as the sky. Almost missing it, I brake amid a chaos of fast hoots, the French as hostile as ever when in cars, out here in nowhere.

I am by the side of an immense field, yes, the Field is still present, and ploughed and hedgeless, as untented as untenanted. It is as if all history has been razed to the furrows to make way for loads of the only local gold: huge misshapen marquees of manure waiting to be spread, proud dung heaps honeyed for an instant by a faint sun. I remember that despite the aureate display by the two kings of France and England, nothing of political advantage or accord was gained on this dismal field, and against the horizon of remote trees I try to envisage the sequence of banquets that ghost it still. *Bisque d'homard, omelette aux truffes, le plateau de fromage* – no, for once the imagination jibs. No priest in his senses would choose this Field for a church fête, let alone a fateful point in history, still less a feast. The Cloth has rotted into the rich soil, the Gold lies in someone's acquisitive vault, the Field is full of shit. Surviving only in hearsay, history at its grandest has reduced itself to compost.

Moving towards the autoroute I try to dredge up Froissart in memory. There is not a lot there. Nor does much of him exist among the facts in books. These men I am following revel in their anonymity, which is why I like them: I am like them, simply; and ignorance, if to little else, is bliss to the imagination. Froissart's presence in the back of the mind is first touched off by place names on signposts. His land is still here; he passed this way. What Berners translated as 'the town of Wissant' is now a friendly resort; mention is made in Froissart's text of the French king departing from Sangatte; at one point Edward III is making for Montreuil-sur-Mer (60 km on the blue signboard), while his marshals moved towards Hesdin, burning and laying waste along my route to the Château de Douriez, where a man of law, or rather a barrister friend, awaits my turning his home into a headquarters for Crécy.

On the autoroute an electronic sign announces an accident between Junctions 28 and 27, so to escape a medieval speed or the equivalent of standstill, whichever is the slower, I plan to turn off on to country roads that snake in and out of natural forms of delay. Now I am at Junction 31, being passed by a lorry packed with Dutch flowers, miles before the stoppage, time on my hands.

Concentrating on the road ahead is to sketch a schoolboy

essay: write a life of Froissart, on one side of the paper only, one hour. Chaucer's senior by a few or several years, Jean Froissart (a Mercedes registered in the Somme cutting in too close for comfort) was born in 1337 or 1333 in Valenciennes, a city in the once independent county of Hainault, now part of France, still shadowed in twentieth-century memory by the passage of two world wars.

Froissart's people were in local business, maybe money-lending, just as Chaucer's were in wine, while Boccaccio's father was a Florentine banker. All three 'poets' (so they viewed their vocation, though it was prose that immortalised two of them) belonged to the rise of the middle class, by and largely for whom the media started to spread beyond court circles. Like Chaucer, Froissart too found his way to court as a young man, his progress accelerating when Philippa of Hainault, England's queen on her marriage to Edward III, took him on in 1361 as a household clerk. The brakes go on – an autoroute toll; coins clatter into the bin. That was the year Chaucer vanished into that seven-year blank which no one will ever explain, a secret beyond knowledge, if not immune to speculation.

England now half his home, Froissart is mainly a flattering versifier to the royals, partly a wide-eyed tourist seeing the sights. He visits the Tower in the flower of cities all, the Savoy, Westminster Palace, not to mention Eltham just off the A2, Leeds Castle on the M20. But mostly he is a nagging seeker-out of material, a polite pest; not so much a historian – the events he values most are current ones – as a newshound without a newspaper. He is a chronicler (I am flashed from behind by a Belgian for hogging the centre lane) subsidised to vaunt the slightly dated exploits of the preposterous vanities of war.

While a team on the way to a fixture waves tipsily from a minibus, in the 1360s our correspondent is nipping over to Europe at intervals, back to Valenciennes, then to Brussels; at any minute he will turn up in Avignon, and after a short whizz to Brittany he descends to Aquitaine where he hobnobs with the Black Prince – here on the A16 the traffic is building up towards the accident ahead. There at Bordeaux (exit Junction 45 on A10) Froissart was 'sitting at table' when Richard II was born in January 1367. 'At that hour Sir Richard de Pontchardon, who was Marshall of Aquitaine at the time, entered and said to me: "Froissart, write down and place on record that her Highness the Princess has been delivered of a fine boy."' It is a moment that across an abyss of time still touches you: a king coming into the world in the near presence of a newspaperman, perhaps a precedent. Seated at his lunch Froissart hears mewling and puking the child into whose mouth Shakespeare will put talk of graves, of worms, and epitaphs, and tell sad stories of the death of kings.

No page in any of the archives divulges much of Froissart. A few statements of his own comprise his biography, the only facts those he volunteers. From such scant references you are at liberty to deduce what you will. Scholars have picked over his life and found only his books. So far I am finding Froissart (millimetres from my wing mirror I am passed by a man angrily agape on his mobile) a busybody. He is poking his nose into other people's business. It is hard to take to his sly way of asking questions of the nobility, hoping to catch his princely prey off balance. Self-cast as anyone's equal, pretending all that interests him is intelligent converse, he is saving up slips of memory or lapses of phrase by the royal person with intent to offer this amalgam to the future as unadulterated history, while also snobbishly licking boots or an occasional arse, as a van from Boulogne carrying a load of fresh fish lacks the power to pass me and falls back.

What did the young Froissart look like? He is to be visualised as small and eager, a lad whose eyes widen in glee at any hint of gossip, who warms his limp handshake at the fire of fame with half a mind to dowse it by inventing the fourth estate, if only to put the other three in their place. I bet he wears a tunic as gaudily naff as an anorak. I warrant he met Chaucer at El Vino the day Geoff beat up that friar in Fleet Street and they had a glass or three together to laugh it off and instruct posterity to forget it. Scribblers never change. Look out for the chip on each shoulder worn as proudly as badges of rank, the eyes that try to hide their need to expose everything in sight and on sight, the breath that exhales a double measure of alcohol with a mixer of confidence as fizzy as it is false, the one hand that taps the table or kneecap or tankard while the other holds the pencil, the sheer style in displaying a singular lack of it. I meet them all the time, on vinous revisits to my now abandoned career as a part-time and nervy and conscience-pricked journo.

With a slight swerve to regain concentration, that articulated vehicle on two levels looking as if all the cars on board are about to fall off the back of the lorry, I promise the autoroute I will never again write for newspapers or I might grow up to be someone like Froissart, whose urgency never flags.

In no time at all, a year later, this tireless enquirer is off to Milan in 1368 for the marriage of Lionel of Clarence, third son of Edward III, to Violante Visconti. This was a ceremony Chaucer also attended; Petrarch too, mentor and friend of Boccaccio. The nuptials last for days but are over in a flash. For our fearless investigator, Rome now looms and fades, Ferrara is next on the signpost, then he's hastening at breakneck speed back to Brussels, taking weeks, where later that year he hears of his patroness Queen Philippa's last hours in England. 'Now let us return to the assembly before Tornehem,' translates Berners, 'and speak of the death of the most gentle queen, most liberal and most courteous that ever was queen in her days, the which was the fair Philippa of Hainault.' The scribbling courtier had lost an ideal as well as a friend.

Thereafter Froissart remains in the Low Countries, his home-land, where in due order he butters up others to earn his bread. Robert of Namur is deranged enough in 1369 actually to commission the *Chronicles*, thus launching his local hack into three decades of sinecure. The no less ingenuous Wenceslas of Bohemia carries on the tradition of subsidising Froissart's relent-less plod towards journalism, until Guy de Châtillon takes over the responsibility of landing the future with a one-man insight team, who has no doubt that all he says or speaks is right, true, just, fine, good: all human life as lived nutshelled into narrative.

A driver in passing glares back with hatred, heating me into hooting in return, and yet they were all good Netherlands men, nothing wrong with Namur for Robert to have been called after it, Wenceslas even a Duke of Luxembourg and Brabant – but what did they think they were doing? They let loose an unspeakable force, destined to speak far too much. They en-couraged this upstart Froissart, whose sole gift was a way with words (too many of them), to report back to the literate (too few of them) on any secret he unveiled about the behaviour of people in the recesses of their privacy. With their patronage these noblemen gave heart to the narcissism that was bound to lure the lesser figure of Froissart, however haunted by ideals, into wanting, demanding, securing, fighting at all costs for the right to publish; as if that too was to win a war and, what was more, a war against them and their interests.

At Junction 27, a succession of lorries masking the slip road, I turn off to avoid the aftermath of that accident. I also avoid thinking of these innocuous valleys burnt to the ground by Edward III, not to mention the Germans of 1940, the Americans of D-Day. The autoroute has bypassed the old barbarisms by substituting death traps of its own. I make an extortionate exit at the booth.

My friend's château is tucked away behind the church, up a narrow lane, camouflaged from the village. It would suit Haig as a headquarters, concealed from enemy air aces by the tall beeches shading it, just large enough to accommodate his staff of half a dozen officers as mannerly at meals as masterly at maps. Solidly second empire in looks, the façade is of a civic pretension that might well conceal a string of mistresses. Pre-1914 wallpaper peels sexily in every room to reveal an anthology of earlier tastes. The proportions are shapely. A flight of stone steps leads up with ceremony to the front door, where an eternal mayor, or indeed field marshal, seems to stand waiting to offer a formal welcome.

But the actuality is an English barrister – who defends criminals in London or with equal relish prosecutes them – waiting with hand outstretched and a wicked grin. His estate is this verdurous square of privacy that cuts off the outside world. He puts a room at my disposal for the night. You would never think war was anywhere within living memory. Yet his plans are for a victory celebration a few days hence. He is about to turn sixty, a decade younger than Froissart at his death.

A local *ouvrier* is already moving among the trees hammering flares into place at intervals. In a barn theatrical lighting is being set up as if to shoot a film. My friend is inviting lots of guests already on high alert, about to invade from England in trains or cars and ships. They have been asked to come not only as themselves but in what he calls on the card 'French dressing': all in duty bound to be someone else. For one night only the whole of Anglo-French history will be theirs to choose from.

As a king or a general or a chronicler I sit at my table thinking of Crécy and how I am going to win it and, if won, how later to report it for posterity, and, if decently reported, how to be sure that my account of it comes anywhere near the truth. I view a map of the Somme on my table. Stroking my upper lip in the absence of Haig's moustache, I plan to launch an offensive on 1 July this very year, 1916, and fingering my chin's lack of Edward III's beard I hope the French cannot catch me up before tomorrow, 26 August 1346. I am summoned to dinner. We eat in the open, sounding off into the night, planning the strategy for these pages, discussing the tactics for his beano.

Next morning I am off to win the war and write the story.

After buying enough provisions at the village shop to feed an army, I drive towards Crécy-en-Ponthieu. About to cross a bridge over the River Authie I halt at a mill race and see the old mill and wonder behind which slit of a window in *The Reeve's Tale* lies the bedroom of the student lodgers who cunningly laid both the daughter and wife of the miller. Though the battlefield is not far in miles, the lascivious recollection of that tale in this setting thrusts the fight at Crécy centuries closer, coitus with the past giving spunk to the present.

The water narrowing into the millstream, I stand on a copy of the very bridge reflected in Chaucer's second line, 'ther goth a brook and over that a brigge'. In *The Canterbury Tales* the story's location is Trumpington, close to Cambridge, a village poeticised by Rupert Brooke who died in the Great War, which devastated these parts of France as crassly as Edward III did, a few years before the story was written in that chamber over Aldgate. The brain races with association.

This unbridled water is hypnotising in its way of suggesting the turbulence of merriment and doom. The act of staring at it stops me in my tracks. I turn off the Clio engine to listen to its gurgling counterpoint on the air, an element which it has sung in since the glaciers melted. I think back to Chaucer's story; this village of Douriez, where I see the story, and that of Deptford, where the story was told, are suddenly one. I forget the events that will climax at Crécy, put war behind me. Yet of course the tale itself is of warfare, albeit domestic, as well as a war of egos between the other pilgrims on the road.

What the Reeve recounts is the ludicrous comeuppance of a cheat of a miller, because his fellow pilgrim the Miller has just told a telling tale about a carpenter, which the Reeve is by trade. When the Reeve finishes, the Cook, at Mine Host's suggestion, has to apologise over telling a story about an innkeeper. The old battles between one human being and another slog to and fro on horseback close by Greenwich. It all feels like home.

Leaning on the rail, looking at the mill, I am suddenly lost to France, research, resolve, the road to Crécy, the effort to slide into Froissart's skin. I am one or other, or both, of the two students who, taking their corn to the Miller to be ground, know at once he will con them. This he achieves by unbridling their horse and setting up his scam as they chase the animal into the wet night. Their revenge, bedroom farce at its comically darkest, is for Aleyn to 'swyve' (not my term) the broad-beamed daughter and Iohn to take ('he priketh harde and depe as he were mad', not my way of putting it) the even more ample wife. A right royal bust-up tops it off. You only have to stare long enough at a real scene to realise it as fiction. That mill tells quite a story.

With satisfaction I climb back into the car. 'There is no one,' Froissart said, 'even among those present on the day, who has been able to understand and relate the whole truth of the matter.' He already knew much about journalism even in its beginnings, if little of his favoured medium of verse.

On his invasion in 1346 of the Cotentin peninsula, Edward ('the king issued out of his ship, and the first foot that he set on the ground, he fell so rudely, that the blood brast out of his nose,' says Berners *pace* Froissart) scarcely knows what is going on, a condition usual to the human mind, easy to share. A desire is rising, not just for the miller's daughter, now turned to nubile dust, but to participate in Edward's knotty difficulties in deciding what to do next: also a shortcut to anxiety as we know it. One answer is to sack any habitation in sight in case it has bows and arrows pointing out of its unglazed windows. The next is to put young crops to the torch lest they feed the enemy when ripe. The third is to rape anyone vaguely female for the hell of it. All else is yob anarchy.

Such acts, in town after town, all the way down the peninsula,

Edward's forces performed – always within sight of the sea, for the fleet followed the army at a wavy remove, collecting rather dim intelligence as they floated on, now and then landing supplies, more disinformation, or reinforcements of rapists. They were the media. They sent the messages.

A day covers this territory, the car (115 b.h.p.) a horse. Spurring it along the routes, mostly byways, chosen by or forced upon Edward by the enemy who, ever at his rear, outnumber him eight to one, feels like fear, like war. One becomes a war buff, mouth dry with longing for adventure, lips moistened only by Froissart's longing to get it down on paper. I sit on vantage points or in cafés, as if lord of one or owner of the other, wondering from which direction the French are coming. A descent on the Somme, expecting the bridges to be destroyed – no, they cross as prettily as pictures – leads to the ford at La Blanchetaque, which Edward perforce used because the French had indeed destroyed the bridges. A spy ('a varlet called Gobin Agace', or so Berners translated) told him that at low tide the water only went up to your waist. But the growth of industry has turned it into a deep canal; from the bank I see my body, weighed down by notepads or chain mail, sink before my gaze as horses white of eyeball churn in the current seawards.

Just upriver there stands an equivalent at Eaucourt-sur-Somme of the camp the English forces have just left. Round a ruined castle, with a ground-down molar of a keep, pulled apart by soldiers from Abbeville to stop its being of service to the English in this or some other fourteenth-century campaign, one or two tents are pitched, striped in brown and white, pennants in a triangular flap of breeze above their octagonal shape. This vision of the Middle Ages under canvas proves only to be the

toolsheds of the faithful restorers who, now absent, are doing up
this wreck of the French heritage.

Hammers are jammed into the mud. Bits of stonework stand
on benches at odd angles. But I at once equate the tents in their
mess, that air of being abruptly abandoned, with the scene at
Airaines, a dozen miles away, 'where [the King] had halted the
troops and ordered them on pain of death', as the translation
goes, 'to do no damage to the town'. The guidebook says that,
rebuilt post-war in dull concrete, here in 1940 1,200 Senegalese
soldiers perished in defence of the town against the panzers. On
the same spot Edward III spent two days in camp.

I dash down D-roads, belaboured by the sense that what is
about to happen has already slipped through my fingers. If I
hurry I can catch it up: a lesson taught only by working for
newspapers. I race into town. Airaines still has the muted misery
of a place that knew the jackboot; resistance is in the air. More
haste is needed to catch the moment before Edward escapes in
the nick of time, upping sticks at dawn, leaving the pursuant
French to find meat on the spits, loaves in the ovens, barrels of
wine, tables ready laid.

Any army needs a halt. I found mine on a railway track, finally
closed in 1973, which had preserved the old Dieppe–Eu line for
walkers. Nobody was walking it. The Clio's hot engine ticked into
cool. I lay in comfort under a birch on a bed of old stones, seeing
the track's curve of quietude as a pilgrim's way now out of use,
watching wildlife, literally bees and birds but much else tinier than
the naked eye, pursuing its ends with no sense that the human
predicament could disturb it. Across a valley of no consequence
swathes of woods offered a prospect of little enough drama.

The absence of time in the scene brought a surge of elation. There was no news. Urgency had ceased to exist. There was a relativity to time I would need (in time) to plumb: the way my men in the fourteenth century used to feel and inwardly measure and ignore time, as opposed to our crass way with the clock. Looking at this eternal nothing of a place at this moment unique to me, I thought that if I could not give myself an impression of how heavy or light time hung for Chaucer and Froissart, here and now, and Boccaccio later in my search but earlier in fact, or of time's particular burden to them – whether a reality, or a punctuation to joy, or simply a pain – I was bound to misunderstand whatever it was that this pilgrimage was urging.

To and fro across the bridges of the Somme, poplars mirrored in its depths, the spirit feels the river's weight on our history from August 1346 to July 1916. Without taking hands off the wheel to check, I sense a knitted brow, persecution gaining, mania not far ahead, a stomach clotted with worry and excitement. I am less in myself than in others, from Edward Plantagenet fighting for England if not for his royal life, via John Berners adding to Calais an impregnable turret and to Froissart nice turns of phrase in English, ending in Douglas Haig subtracting thousands of English lives like mine on that first dawn of the Somme campaign.

That evening I make an incursion along the Somme estuary to Le Crotoy, which Edward's outriders burn to the ground in the search for provisions on the run-up to Crécy. A bit thirsty I look for bars round the harbour, where Froissart says the king's marshals 'found in the haven many ships and barks charged with wines of Poitou, pertaining to the merchants of Saintonge and of Rochelle', but now the haven has largely silted up. There is a marina packed tight with yachts that can escape to sea only at high tide. The marshals send the wine back to Edward's army camped a few miles away, liquid courage for the troops. On the front I raise a glass, not from the environs of Poitiers but not bad, to the good luck of being here and now and myself: more than enough of a toast.

In this resort on the far edge of history, I stay a night before battle commences. In essence it is a miniature of seaside holidays from childhood: a curve of quay, a length of promenade, shops parading back into the quiet of residential streets, sand between the toes, salt on the lips. A nice old slattern gives me a room. From my window extend the salt marshes, sandbanks flocked by seabirds and sheep. Flat lands ease into a flatter sea. The outlook, dissolving in a haze to a ghost of St Valery-sur-Somme on the opposite shore, seems as passive as history, infinite, indefinite.

Not much of old Le Crotoy survived all the sacks. A stroll reveals a bulging fragment of a stone wall, with glimpses within of a bourgeois garden. It is a scrap of a dungeon that was Joan of Arc's last lodging in 1431. From here she was taken to the stake in Rouen by the English whose forebears only a couple of generations earlier are setting fire in my presence to this nice little town with its shoal of restaurants facing the very sea that serves up the fish on the twenty-euro menu.

I am as little able as Froissart to report so world-shaking an event as that battle at Crécy. He wasn't there either, being at the time a lad coping with puberty in the back streets of Valenciennes. He was as dependent on an earlier chronicler called Jehan le Bel as I am on him. Nor was le Bel present on the field of Crécy. But he knew people who were. I am hearing voices at two or even three removes. I have no reason to suppose that, like me now in age, Froissart in youth visited the landscape to envisage the detail of the battle; but he no doubt did. A reporter's instinct, if not necessarily a historian's duty, is to view the scene of the crime. With this in mind I can parallel Froissart's feelings. He and I are as good as contemporaries.

Next morning, thinking of war with the usual mix of horror and high spirits, I drive the car over bumpy ground into shade not a mile from the battlefield at Crécy. I stare at my maps, my back against a trunk in this forest, spacious with glades under canopies of beech and oak, where Edward's army spent a last night before the battle. As I lay out a picnic on an unread newspaper, the mind drags back to the pace of things then: that long trek down the Cotentin peninsula that preceded Crécy, relying for intelligence on a fleet tracking the army onshore, receiving in my tent the bustle of couriers with variant stories of what lies ahead, sending out advance parties which report back garbled with contrariety.

On this spot, over this picnic, camped a great English army: gobbling torn-off fistfuls of *baguette*, ham folded in the fingers, tomato bitten into and dripping seeds, *pâté de campagne* thick with garlic, swilling a heady red wine, listening to the speed of cars whizzing past the silence. Even their dull roar, surprisingly enough, echoes Crécy in 1346: the first fight in the west in which violent noise was component if not effective. The original cannons boomed, herald of the howitzer, hint of the nuclear.

I lie back in an effort to relax on the bulge of roots of an oak the size of a warship. Vaguely wondering if modern war and the modern media were born in this same breath of time, I am abruptly taken short. On the eve of battle I dash into under-

growth, pulling at my belt. Trousers down, tickled by under-
growth, I have to squat, eyes gazing into the infinity of
tomorrow, hoping to survive it, expelling a blast of wet shit.
I use, with irony, the newspaper torn up, full of today's events,
full of itself, ink still smudgeable.

At the battlefield the French have done the English victory
proud by building an observation platform. Wide stairs lead to
the point of vantage, where stood the windmill under the sails of
which Edward III is supposed to have surveyed the battle, if not
commanded it. The evidence is slight, the appeal strong. In a
sidepack, which pulls on a shoulder that in turn weighs down the
ankle, I have a wodge of photocopies in different typefaces from
various centuries of varying descriptions of the Battle of Crécy.
All are translated (as said), or transformed (as implied), from the
original Froissart, who took his account from le Bel (as noted),
himself no eyewitness. Truth is anyone's guess.

Yet, if you gaze out from this position of strength, the whole
shambles seems so obvious. Nobody is here this deserted afternoon, or indeed within sight, the sun lowering. Did that sun
blind the French advance or was it raining too hard? Reports
differ. I am alone on the battlefield, in sole charge of history.
Looking towards Abbeville, giving ear to my scouts, I have the
battle plan in front of me, an orientation sketched under glass in
fake medieval scripts and symbols. Feeling tense, strung tight as a
bow, I am personally taking part in, am partly responsible for, an
event very famous, and this time it might go wrong – time plays
tricks, history need not always repeat itself. I know just what it is
to be, tongue drying, knees jellying, a master of my fate and am
weakened by a surge of pity for those not yet dead who have an
hour left to live.

The spots of rain that start falling do not improve the quality of the photocopies. Soon I can hardly read what happens next. The words blur. Water drips off the leaden sentences as the first wave of the French, in a plod more threatening than a charge, move in an undulating series of ranks across several fields, planted with corn, towards our position. The Genoese archers up front have to cope with the strings of their crossbows getting soaked by the downpour, and all is confusion, with the mounted knights pounding behind them, and I am letting loose my longbowmen who stand behind me, in a reshoot of a costume drama, showering with arrows those mercenaries from the land of Boccaccio. The arrows slam home at the rate of three per minute per man.

What of the enemy rear? The cream of the French aristocracy dancing up behind in all their tournament togs, at once assuming treachery ahead, rides roughshod through the stricken Genoese, in a cavalry charge that imitates, in stupidity and glory, countless others that are to decorate the future of European warfare. Under a continuous rain of arrows, in the continuous rain, horses crumple to death with savage neighs of agony, knights topple off and flounder heavily in the rapidly forming mud, and our own army is scarcely dented. The lads stand firm on this prominence with the steady bravura to let the successive waves of Frenchmen commit suicide on their spears, swords, daggers; while on the sidelines, for the first time ever, presaging, I repeat, howitzers on the Western Front in the Great War, with the impact of surprise created, I reiterate, by the atom bomb seemingly as long ago as Crécy, the first crude cannons bang and smoke and hurl out balls little more hurtful than the stones boys throw.

I am not only almost the victor, I am the first reporter on the scene. Unless you count the four evangelists, I have got myself the first exclusive in history. I can tell it the way it was. I am seeing it happening in front of my very eyes.

Yet – as I stuff the sodden photocopies back into my satchel – I know I am totally unreliable. I never saw it all. The little I saw was hardly any of it. As king I was pleased to win, pour out the wine, bury the dead, feast, empty the bowels, raise a cheer. As reporter I am haunted for six centuries by having missed not just the point but the essence. Yet I have one duty left. It is to tell everyone, particularly the dead, what happened. Out of the bag that contains my despatches I take the one remaining dry account. Still no one is up here in the eyrie or down there on the battlefield. I can shout to my heart's content. I can tell it from the rooftops. I am the town crier, the messenger panting into headquarters on a horse frothing at the bit, in the rapid process of transforming my brain into a fledgling broadsheet. I print the words on the air.

'On the Friday, as I said before,' said Berners in the name of Froissart,

the king of England lay in the fields, for the country was plentiful of wines and other victual, and if need had been, they had provision following in other carts and carriages. That night the king made a supper to all his chief lords of his host and made them good cheer; and when they were all departed to take their rest, then the king entered into his oratory and kneeled down before the altar, praying God devoutly, that if he fought the next day, that he might achieve the journey to his honour: then about midnight he laid him down to rest, and in the morning he rose betimes and heard mass . . .

Then the king leapt on a hobby, with a white rod in his hand, one of his marshals on the one hand and the other on the other hand: he rode from rank to rank desiring every man to take heed that day to his right and honour. He spake it so sweetly and with so good countenance and merry cheer, that all such as were discomfited took courage in the seeing and hearing of him. And when he had thus visited all his battles, it was then nine of the day: then he caused every man to eat and drink a little, and so they did at their leisure. And afterward they ordered again their battles: then every man lay down on the earth and by him his salet and bow, to be the more fresher when their enemies should come.

As I read aloud to the sky the Berners translation of Froissart – not the modern ones, too drab and lifeless, not the Victorian, too prosy – the scene of the fight arises from the vitality in the words. Bright is their ring. How they lure the battle out of the back of the mind, how the images surge forward like troops at their touch. For some reason I feel very close to all three of my writers here at Crécy. Like them I am all alone without even an army, except of nerves, genes, pulses, muscles, brawn, the rest. Yet by reporting it I am as much in charge of the event as those who prompted it.

Only now, standing above it waiting, is it about to occur. At this moment Chaucer is four, Froissart seven, and Boccaccio, so far away as not to notice, thirty-one. I am well on the way to twice their combined ages, up to the ears in their differing wisdoms, half a dozen centuries more advanced in science, but the game's the same. Like Edward III, like Philip VI, like the Black Prince, I am fighting this battle, first to release aggressions, next to supply needs, and last to do justice to ideals. Like Froissart I am offering posterity an account of it. Crécy is a quarrel with my next-door neighbour which I write to the local paper about, a tiff with my lover which goads me into scribbling her a note of outrage, an accident on the motorway that is nobody's fault but the system's. It is also plainly murder.

As I walk I feel needless bones massed under my feet. This war that wipes out any activity worth the name of life in this swathe of France is to go on for a century. Not even a sketch of a treaty occurred for fifteen years until in 1360 the kings met at a hamlet called Brétigny, within sight of the twin towers of Chartres, to sign a paper committing both sides to peace. Almost within months, as a way of finally putting out to kennels the dogs of war, the treaty lost bite. Meanwhile, and for good, I feel ashamed to be a journalist. I want to write no more, except to explain why (not directly) I want to write no more.

Even before the start of this journey I had been possessed by the fourteenth-century obsession with death. It was more a part of life than life was. They were persistently troubled, these people, at every level in all the classes. All recent histories had quotes that struck both fright and fellow-feeling into a modern heart. 'A general feeling of impending calamity hangs over all,' said a Dutch scholar in 1924. 'Perpetual danger prevails everywhere.' If you did not lead an anguished life, you were not alive, there was no hope, Satan had the edge on Jesus. An American in 1978 found her study of the fourteenth century 'consoling in a period of similar disarray'. There was no sense of an assured future, she added. Their lives were not even worth their death.

Also there was a slip into an ice age, which grew perceptible in

1303. The summers were as short and hot as tempers. Otherwise little grain came up in Sweden, the Baltic froze across, children were eaten, the poor in Poland gorged on bodies cut down from gibbets. The cold lasted four centuries into better times, but it cut Froissart's poor Europe to the quick.

People viewed their fate as naturally unhappy. Evils existed only to mount in horror, until death might or might not relieve you of them. Governments were royally distant, but as of right stole whatever money or service was yours to give, either making you pay for a war or fight in it. Outside the cruelty of society lurked the brigands, either a threat or at your throat, preying on your woman or child or larder. Insecurity sharpened when it grew ever more obvious that the Hundred Years War was your lifetime, having been your father's, now handed on to your children. Warfare was chronic. The end of the world was continuously nigh.

'That conflict between the reach for the divine and the lure of earthly things,' said that 1976 historian, 'was to be the central problem of the Middle Ages.' Well, the media was our church; we attended its daily rites, fearing to be left behind, miss the message. Nobody refused to attend this church, go on television, or be interviewed for a paper. Those who ran the media, the arch-priests of the business, were huffy when anyone said no or did not confess or bend the knee. I thought how the actual churches, in our society's psyche at least, were gasping for breath at the margins, while how little of value to the spirit appears on prime time or in final editions. The media conflates divine and earthly so casually that none of us any longer knew the difference. It was as though we had done with the soul.

★　　★　　★

To the Abbaye de Valloires, now a hotel where the night is to be
spent, the noblest of the French dead were taken by Edward III.
He gave them a burial in a propriety of environ that solemnifies
almost to nonsense the reasonless losses of war. In this narrow
valley of the Authie, a mere trickle, the Abbaye is hugely
dominant, vast silent cloisters, corridors the width of a salon
and the length of a nave. The air of sepulchral gloom, as I settle
into a suite of rooms that on bed or chaise longue would sleep
half a dozen, is lifted by distant outbursts of chatter, an echoing
uprush of giggles under some vault far away.

Outside a towering window that overlooks a perspective of
formal gardens, Napoleon is prancing across a lawn, slapping
his calfskin leg in a paroxysm of self-aggrandisement. A couple
of ladies of the court, attired in full-length gowns ballooning
to the ankle, looking less like belles than handbells, point at
the Emperor and their laughter rings out. A stunning scene: far
from vanishing, Napoleon performs a little jig, removes his
cocked hat and bows low to the ladies and suggests, in the
slightly immaculate English of not too bad a school, that a
bumper of fizz in his room before the party may well not
come too much amiss with one and all. I half knew it, of
course – he is less a revenant than a guest tricked out in
yesteryear at our host's request. It is the night of the barrister's
sixtieth.

My own disguise appears dingy by comparison. In slight panic
I wonder how many Voltaires or Matisses or de Gaulles will be
overplaying their pretensions in a vernacular sandwiched in
accent between golf course and law court. Changing into my
peasant outfit, I am full of regret for opportunities not taken. I
really could be someone else. This might prove my last chance.

Meanwhile the sun is going down all over Europe, and I shall be late for the party.

How does a peasant think? The rim of the beret is biting into my brow like a prejudice. On the way a flock of wayside fowl quack in fright into the air. Gazing immemorially into the woods as if they were my roots, I rub horny hands down the thighs of my corduroys. With a bit of forethought I could have been Jean Cocteau, bringing a sheaf of my drawings to the party. Or as Maurice Chevalier thanking heaven for little girls. Or Marshal Foch winning the first of the wars to end wars. Or Mitterrand slyly stroking an illicit breast while asserting the legality of pan-European ideals.

Little does our host know, but I have really come as Froissart, though I may look like a rustic; Froissart himself was prone to hide behind another identity, even it if was only geniality personified. But in thinking over this matter of disguise, I was not prepared to come as someone as laughably not myself as a chronicler, with a flattish chef-like hat of unfashionable design and a paunch pillowed into a bulge.

The mood of the party establishes itself as timeless. Stand in the shadows, and you can see the whole of French history before you in panorama and in caricature. Gilded by the flicker of the lamplight a knight or courtier or jester is moving at a clip towards the refreshment tent. A blue film is in the making in that corner under the steps where an aristocrat, about to be guillotined, is bending with salacity over a girl occupying a gap-legged limbo between a chambermaid and a cancan dancer. Seeing in the dusk someone half-known dressed as someone else not quite identifiable lends him or her an authority they never enjoyed when last seen in an inner London suburb or on a country walk in Kent. A

Clapham housewife looks better as a Montmartre tart or more
real as a Neuilly mistress. A civil servant cuts a dash as Talleyrand.
People take off into themselves by becoming someone else, not
acting a part, but releasing an inner part by outing into a disguise.

Among the fancy-dressed I keep looking for the real Froissart.
A number of beards flaunt themselves in the flickering half-
darkness with oddly costumed bodies below them. None seems
to have the required stature. I am victim to everyone's assump-
tion that celebrities are by definition tall, darkly sexy and
handsomely mantled with authority. God forbid that when I
locate him Jean Froissart will be inferior to the images, in statue,
engraving, prose, or the back of my mind, which admiration has
of him as a founding father.

Next morning nothing can proceed further without finding out
where and how Jean Froissart spent his boyhood and why and in
what quarter he met his end. I need the span of the man. I
require to know of him, privately, almost what I know of myself;
or at least to sense it, to suss out a guess.

From his minimal biography I know that Froissart spent the
two extremes of his life, the earliest as a boy, the last and longer as
an ancient, in the same area, in Hainault, not many miles east of
where I stand.

To my surprise the road into a town called Les Andelys
advertises a medieval pageant. Also on the fringe of town a
mighty ruin of a castle glowers on a cliff over the Seine. At first I
suspect this to be another dead town rebuilt post-war in the
concrete of despair. But as I shop for a picnic glimpses of a less
recent past survive in back streets. Hunched under a tower
block, a cottage; in a desert of development, a villa shuttered: as

if generations too old to exist are still clinging to life in those small structures, shards of people who go back through the Industrial Revolution all the way to the plague. Meanwhile I debate about the several cuts of ham in a *charcutier*'s window.

Somewhere behind the street scene rattles a tambourine. I am at once on my mettle. A trumpet flourishes, a rehearsal of the past is in progress. A knight in full rig will suddenly dash through the square and smite an opponent in Chaucer's Smithfield. With vague expectancy a number of flak jackets move into place on the pavements, along with a tide of cut-price jeans, a few prams with babies moribund under the canopies, a pair or two of working blues from the last century, and three or four youths identified as sentient only by a phone or earpiece clapped to their heads. On the mouths of the mothers lipstick is the one disguise vivid enough to brighten the morning, which is abruptly aroused by a striking up, a dancing, a prancing, as a procession rounds a corner out of the fourteenth century – and enters time.

At the forefront a few monsters on stilts descend writhing on the women with prams, who ape fright with screams more like sex than terror. Behind them, to general delight, bats, basilisks, dragons, or locals dressed as them, sway and stride into a crowd halfway through the drudge of shopping for lunch. Drums beat at the rear, bagpipes squeak in front, ranks of girls in harmony twirl and bow and grin, squires in good old armour and churls in chain mail kick their heels as they await their turn to march. From nowhere the formation hoots and skirls and bangs its way into the here and now.

And it all seems to have been put on for Froissart. It is to raise the flag of his faith in the chivalry that flaps on every page, and for once, buoyed by this arousal of the past by locals descended

from it, I scramble into his mind, humbly. I am Froissart hearing
the flute that blows the sad last shriek of the pageant. I become
him looking with suspicion at salmon in jelly, him buying a slice
of underdone beef in a shop where after the procession the
daughter has shed her costume to help her dad at the counter,
Froissart picking a traditional bread, him grasping by the neck a
Loire wine. It flushes over me, this being someone else, as hot as
an embarrassment, as I pay up.

And I am a reporter again. I work for the local paper. The old
itch returns. My copy must be in by lunch. I detest what I cannot
resist. Stomach cramp threatens, strain stirs like the onset of a
headache, but I am in the grip of a manic need to know, enquire,
describe, reveal, expose. Graphic phrases whizz through the
mind at twenty-four frames a second, my camcorder eyes zoom
in and out, my manners hit bottom as I push through the
bystanders, hands as clenched as steel, craving to suck in and then
puff out the cleverness of the story, the facts in all their dubiety,
the scandal that is bound to be the truth.

The car now feels as confining as my desk once did. As if
trying to catch up that deadline I drive out of town towards
Froissart's birthplace.

Years as a hack passed like this. After a night of effort at a
typewriter, I used to see dawn edging into the window without
a printable word on paper. To whip the mind into the missing
tingle I drank whisky at an hour when most people were
sleeping off hangovers. I paced at random, knees weak with
failure. From the shelf I took down books to remind me of
permanence. A black nemesis lurked behind the brightening of
the light outside. Ruthless editors were sleepily pulling up their

socks. At breakfast they ensured their spectacles were as meti-
culously polished as the prose they expected to receive from me
within the hour. A chauffeur motored them towards my doom.
Commissionaires saluted them on the steps of a headquarters of
the press as I gazed for the last time at my empty page.

And then without a second's warning I hunched over the
keyboard and without a trace of anxiety or haste I tapped out in
no time a thousand or so words to keep fish and chips in business
the day after tomorrow, as well as to enlighten a readership of
millions. It was done.

The idea that happiness might exist flickered through some
rear compartment of the mind. Then, bursting at the seams with
self-respect, I revised the piece with a sure hand to the scent of
frying bacon, I ate sumptuously, poured down hot tea, lit the
night's ninety-ninth and finest cigarette, and just as editors had
with due pomp taken their seats at the power of their desks,
poised to sack me for truancy, I was on the phone to the copy-
takers, dictating genius by the mouthful.

In a square opposite a church at Valenciennes a hotel frontage
unfolds in a series of tall shuttered windows. In the quiet street I can
park outside. The dim vestibule is deserted as if sound-proofed.

From far away down a tiled corridor a click of high heels
approaches very fast but taking ages. A woman of passing allure,
if a touch more *laide* than *jolie*, looks me up and down, as though
the cat, which wheedles round her legs, has brought me in. Have
I reserved? There is a film festival in Valenciennes, *vous savez*.
There are important world *cinéastes* staying in the hotel. *L'hôtel
est tout complet.* She looks down on me, beringed hands folded on
handouts about the films to be shown.

No room? Well, *en principe*, no, but there is one without a bath in the basement. I embrace the offer to her instant displeasure, while scanning the range of flimsy entertainment which looks as polyglot as it is pretentious. The high heels tap a protest as she takes away my passport to imprison it in a safe. I am no English milord here to bolster the local economy. Still less am I present to launch a movie into oblivion or rescue Froissart from it by writing a screenplay.

My room has a small window gazing upward at a sharp angle into a small muddle of garden as oblong as a television screen. Bracketed under the low ceiling is indeed a television set pointed downwards at the bed like a closed-circuit window. Overhead, back and forth, click the busy castanets of high heels on a tiled floor. Her activity is hard to identify, but ceaseless. The mind taps with nervous fantasy. At one moment she is reverently carrying to the wash sheets soiled by Martin Scorsese or a towel used by Francis Ford Coppola to mop up spilt milk. Then she is clattering into the distance to hand Ingmar Bergman, with an erotic curtsey, his keys. Then she is pattering in an approach to ecstasy as Brigitte Bardot bends down to stroke her cat. The stress of her going to and fro over my head transfers itself to my brain as a message, rapped out with the urgency of morse, that she has the future of communications in her hands. Only I am the half-buried present.

But I have a chance of the past under my feet. In the soil of Valenciennes, under the cheap tiles, lies the birthplace if not the body of Jean Froissart.

Who was he, what was he like, how did he get the idea, how did he throw off the burden of his commercial forebears, what started him off, what went on motivating him, why did he take so much trouble, if it wasn't just an appetite for the unknowable that lay beyond the facts? Froissart starts the hopeless search for verity as well as veracity, is curious, asks questions, presses people not to lie to him, needs to know, knows how to tell, and all at once he is attending a film festival on expenses to report it the way it is for posterity.

Though everyone up to the nineteenth century execrated his reliability as a historian, they still pinched his research and perpetuated his myths. All he wanted was to say it like it was, to be the reflective mirror in which he kept an eye on the pen in his own hand, trying for the truth with continuous effort, but all the time aware that he was failing it. Only the most arrogant of journos believe that only theirs is the accurate report leading to the correct conclusion. I have a desire to report Froissart's natal city with all his qualities brought to bear on a place he knew and I have never seen. To start I get up off the bed and at once give my temple a sharp blow on a forgotten corner of the television set that hangs from the ceiling. I do not see stars.

By repute Valenciennes is a place from which nothing (except a film festival) can be expected. In the last century shells or bombs have twice wrought havoc with it. It lies at the heart of the overtipping slagheaps of old French mines that by their very industry helped keep wars going; self-destruction was innate. Also Froissart's birthplace has suffered more damage from the bellicosity vaunted by his *Chronicles* than anywhere Chaucer knew, even London, not to say Boccaccio's Florence. All trace of him as a boy has been wiped out at least twice. The medieval remnants that could contain a touch of his spirit, or offer a view of the townscape familiar to him, are the wooden houses that

clustered in the old city, until twice destroyed in bombing by
each side at both ends of the last war, in the advance of 1940 and
the retreat of 1944. All is gone, save in photos. In the souvenir
shops the Great War postcards, though printed only a dozen
years before my birth, look at least as old as the fourteenth
century.

I make heart in mouth for the Place Froissart, expecting him
to be there as if we have made an appointment. I have yet to
form an image of this middle-class prototype who as a poet
sucked up to the mighty, neither jesting nor jousting at court,
just eyeing its dubious doings from not quite behind the arras,
revealing their courtly capers to the world, not to put them
down, but to give their activities a sheen of nobility which only a
toady can confer: Froissart is that secret addict of privilege who
pretends to be a democrat.

I long to see his likeness. The Michelin guide says there is a
statue in the square.

The square – long and of good proportions, given to commerce, the law, municipal offices, printers – is a rectangle sloping
upwards to a sculpture of the seated chronicler at its zenith. He
takes centre stage, whiter than white. His monumental figure is
ringed to his rear by a semicircle of linked pillars, on which runs a
frieze recording the names of other sons of Valenciennes by a
long chalk less glorious. Nymphs and shepherds swell a bas-relief
under the arches. Echoing them to the life, teenage boys and
girls are draped on the curve of benches, as cool as statues,
reading paperbacks not written by Froissart.

Our star reporter's shoes stand on a plinth quite a few blocks
of stone higher than my head. Viewed from below he is a huge
man, more clothes than flesh; the sculptor knew less how to

carve personality than drapes. He wears stone vestments so churchy, so weighty, as to bring him in, if you were running for a scoop, a poor last. I do not want the founder of investigative journalism to be dressed up as a petrified vicar. I try to imagine the human body beneath the lifeless folds. A particularly un-erotic curve of marble laps over his private parts. The hand that penned the *Chroniques* is itching to rise from the trammels of the cope, either to rewrite the last version of Crécy or to give a blessing to a girl poring over history homework on the bench below. For this is where youth comes after school to smoke and dabble in gossip and make history and plan the future, more or less, with differences slighter than you think, just as Froissart did.

I look up at his face: impenetrable, the hair too long for my liking, besides which it has a flat hat on it, a medieval beret that betokens wisdom; Erasmus used to wear one. The nose sticks out distinctly, not a nose you would wish to go to bed with, more a snoring type of nose. His posture is that of a man who knows it all, but that may be the fault of the sculptor, named Jacquet, no doubt a romantic whose only interest in the four-teenth century was to carve profit out of it in the nineteenth. Those bald eyes will not mind what they are gazing blindly out on. But, I abruptly realise, they will see his very world as he established it, a sane polite world, a world of well-enforced discipline, the world that Prosper Merimée, he who chronicled the altogether sexier affairs of Carmen, was still enjoying in 1856 when he, as a French minister of culture with a good lunch in front or inside of him, unveiled this statue.

I walk round the square, Froissart's mercantile values reflected in the present. Small businesses line it on all sides. At the bottom end facing the statue at a remove Meubles Ramoux ('*bonnes affaires pendant les travaux*'), Constructions Immobilières du Nord ('*comment être bien chez soi*'), Val Plan ('*copy service*'), Pierre Durieux ('*Assurance et Finance*'), then an *imprimerie* looking up to him; two accountants (Didier Quoibion, Pierre Telle) with brass plates, the weight of sober consultancy growing heavier by the moment, by two houses side by side in single occupation, but then to raise the tone for Froissart a courtyard houses the headquarters of HEC-BDL, Societé d'Expertise Comptable et Commissariat aux Comptes (five brass plates), while the monster of a Second-Empire building at Froissart's back houses Unité Telemarketing, several Huissiers de Justice Associés, a firm of architects, Les Boutiques ('*club emploi*'), and at the farthest corner, diagonal to Froissart's stony stare, stands a closed café called Sixteen, not much fun.

In fact he bosses the square. On his pedestal Froissart sits as smug as a proprietor of the present.

The ankle has had enough of research. It drags me down the street past bars deserted but for television, bypassing the hotel in case cineastes are blocking the vestibule. Dusk has supervened to make the city look worth exploring. I am feeling my way through a guidebook. The Auberge du Bon Fermier, a survivor from a mere couple of centuries after Froissart, therefore well in character if not strictly in period, charges me a lot for a pastis and indeed for its past. A suit of armour stands at the bar as if waiting for a drink. Beams are lean-to, the swing door to the bar is an allotment fence badly tacked together from driftwood, the charm of the place lying in the imminence of its crumbling to dust. I ask for a menu. I sit looking at a portrait of a partridge waiting to be shot.

The delay is long. I feel for that hollow knight, as I do for

Froissart, in his stony gown, undergoing a painful wait for royal attention when wanting to present Richard II with a copy of his book, which extolled the ideal of being dressed in armour. Eventually *le patron* appears and sits me at a rough-hewn table for at least six. On one wall a tapestry hangs in a faded blaze of *l'amour* among meadows florally medieval. I work through a healthy meal Froissart might have ordered: salad of sharp greens, salmon sauced with sorrel, carrots, spinach, bread crustily brown, just the roughage a chronicler needs. A low-key Vivaldi provides the musak.

At this moment elsewhere in Valenciennes, men whose methods spring from Froissart are busy promoting their wares. The curtain has just fallen on films that are masterpieces only in the marketing. In cinemas all over town the egos of their makers are being clapped into the spotlight. They are cheered by the municipal great and good, as much for documentaries eating into the alkaline assumptions of their hosts as for gangster movies that spray bullets all over the mayoral party in the front row. In their speeches the cineastes will not mention Froissart, even as they strut the stage of his birth. Unaware of his name, these toffs of communication will assume his non-existence. Scorsese got the best room in the hotel. Bardot was promised all the privacy she never wanted. Their lavatories are en suite. Ingmar Bergman is favoured by a balcony, as well as by the none too *jolie laide*. The suit of armour gleams a reproach at my absurdity as I pay the bill.

I wish the musak had been Guillaume de Machaut. But maybe his pieces have too earthy a rhythm. They pound a bit too hard for ease. A pair of sharp voices slicing into the eardrums is not the best accompaniment to a good dinner. Waiting for management to return my credit card, I think of all the love there in the fourteenth-century lyrics. Every syllable aches with pining, not to mention the tense pull of the tune. Even trying to recall the words to mind is a pain. It comes back like heartburn.

> *Mais votre douce figure*
> *Votre exquise beauté que j'adore*
> *Et votre noble personne*
> *Parée de charmants atours*
> *En pleurs tiennent nuit et jour,*
> *Sans qu'il en éprouve joie,*
> *Mon coeur qui vit dans une tristesse*
> *Dont il ne peur guérir.*
> *Hélas, Dame de haut prix.*

I almost hear the tune. Without being cut in half my credit card is served me on a platter.

On the way out, as I stand vacantly at the urinal, verses swim before me. They are the same shape as those just remembered from Machaut. They are attached to the lavatory wall and read as follows:

> *Dans ce lieu peu confortable*
> *Mais pourtant indispensable*
> *Tenez-vous comme à table*
> *Faites que la lunette*
> *Soit aussi propre que votre assiette*
> *Et qu'il ne reste aucune miette*
> *Car c'est ici que tombent en ruines*
> *Avec odeur et triste mine*
> *Toutes les merveilles de la cuisine.*

Hoping I am late or early enough to slip into the hotel unseen, I slink from the silent street into an inferno of noise. From a saloon next to reception arise the well-known shouts and screeches of a children's party. Some of these kids are grown women whose hairdos are as high as the heels the hotel landlady has aped them in wearing. The boys have broken voices that are like automatic weapons, gunning a stream of witticisms at point-blank range into made-up faces that crumple in a scream. I know at once where I am. This, narrowly funnelled into the provincial hindquarters of a small hotel in Valenciennes, is a deafening echo of the hype of Cannes at festival time, the Lido at Venice on the eve of the Golden Lion award, the Oscars writ small in a Hollywood drunkenly shrunk to the size of a backstreet beano. It will all end in tears.

Back in my stuffy room the only escape is that set that keeps hitting me. It now does it again as I step into pyjamas. When the lights are out and sleep comes hard, the red pupil of stand-by is a glimmer on the ceiling that seems to be a sign from on high. A click, I am past prime time, well into habit, aka research. In my hand I have a black oblong of power armed with buttons.

Up comes an advert about starlings eating cherries that end up potted, a parlour game called *Who is Who* in which everyone claps in unison with a host called Bertrand who imitates noise to such pointless effect that hilarity greets his every sally, a trio of channels embedded in fiscal matters involving a drop in the value of the euro, a football match raging between Paris (3) and Bordeaux (nil), a weather forecast for Belgium, a contradictory forecast of French weather, a prediction of the storms Germany must expect, a child in an American sitcom who is attacking his parents, a man from *Libération* rousing by rhetoric a press conference to a spurious indignation over a local issue that deeply compromises liberty, if not equality not to say fraternity, news from New York devoting a third of the screen to the deaf and dumb. That's about it.

I turn it off. There is a blessed silence that also seems damned. From very far away a slight rhythm edges into my mind, growing into a pulse that becomes a tap and before I realise I am suffering from a headache it is directly overhead, hammering with a drum of interference into my brain; without pause or apology it recedes, bearing with it the loads of wine glasses imprinted with lipstick, the half-eaten snacks, the leftovers that are the autographs of the party that has now dispersed into the superior bedrooms, where once more they are soiling the sheets that will tomorrow set the heels and the gossip clacking.

I have failed to find the lad Jean in his own town. The boy must be elsewhere. Perhaps I need more time. I caught a glimpse in a derelict square of a fountain meant to remember him but not working, no huge fling of sun-glittered water prisming the heavens that boys like, just a dirty old bowl. Valenciennes has gone back a long distance since he was born hereabouts. He wouldn't be seen dead in it, but he would have liked the railway station. It still looks very important, as if it led some-where.

The boy born here took half a century to become the old man a few miles to the east.

When I tap the bell on the desk to check out, the high heels tap a final message: *félicitations* on leaving our town, not very *bon voyage*. As I leave, the rearview mirror shows that the Wednesday market covers two squares and runs into several streets, sketching as it recedes all the swag I have missed – oysters, scarves, luggage, cheese, handbags, frocks, beef, stockings, binliners, oranges, marinated anchovies, lavatory brushes, bread – the immemorial essential of a very old town in France, its commerce, the mercantile base of the chronicler's forebears: the market, the market! But it is too late to turn back. Searches generate their own urgency. Froissart might die in retirement before I reach him.

So by now he is all ready to finish (but when exactly) Book I? It is long, and it vividly contains Crécy, which was fought when he was a teenager there in Valenciennes. At this point his patrons put their heads together. Shall we let him go on? Will it cost us too much? What has he got to offer? All over his homeland men of power are waiting to trap Froissart into holy orders. They are saying that nobody will believe his accounts unless he has a measure of divinity thrust upon him. That will buy him time, they imply. That will keep him quiet. He can write to his heart's content and bother us no more, except with dedications, if not a touch of bias in favour of our chosen causes.

The pro-English Robert de Namur began the process of patronising the *Chronicles* in 1369. When for whatever reason he withdrew his august approval, his place was taken by the pro-French Wenceslas of Bohemia (son of the blind king who blundered to his death at Crécy), so Froissart perforce sat down to a labour not of love but of rewriting the *Chroniques* to put the French effort in a fairer light. Impartiality was ever the aim of a good reporter. In any case the French connection eased his passage in and out of France in the dignified chase for material.

Thus the hefty remainder of his life was spent as a nominal priest in Belgium. Soon after Valenciennes, with a sense of fast-forwarding in time from infancy to senility, I cross unnoticed the unremarkable border between the two countries. Thanks to the beneficence of Guy de Châtillon, I have been granted the living of Estinnes-au-Mont in Brabant. I proceed down the street that drives towards somewhere even less interesting and swing into the square, obviously a flattened version of the old churchyard. Fragments of gravestones, from funerals conducted by successors of Froissart, having been dug from their spots, are propped against the church walls in ranks that look like a mass execution.

No one is parked in the vast space left by this massacre. A dead bar is unwelcoming, a cross between French café and English pub at the depressed end of hospitality's scale. I wonder why I am here. The ankle, back in force after its long drive, makes heavy going of rising to the '*mont*' on which the church that is now Froissart's living stands. The church is shut and locked and idle and unwanted and ugly.

I shall have to make the best of this first parish. Yet no parishioners are in sight. A succession of farms line the rivulet that runs alongside the Rue Grande. The outsides have the look of places that have nobody inside. Blank walls guard barns. Nothing is shut up; everything is shut off. Belgium has shut down. I think of it with jubilance as Froissart did coming into town. It is a boringly ideal place to settle down in peace and start revising a chronicle that will grasp the fourteenth century neck and crop. The town hall is drably beflagged. The place has standstill built into it. Everyone is laid up indoors on a fattening diet of television.

However, contrary to trend in Estinnes, I glimpse a promotion pinned to a telegraph pole. It flaps in an idle breeze. The Taverne le Froissart is throwing a party but rain has washed off

the orange highlighter than spells out the date. Any minute now
I might be missing something. The venue is down the Rue
Grande and by my watch it's noon, high time for a shindig.
Where's Froissart? These rustics springing loonily out of the
blank outbuildings, crazy to make exhibitions of themselves
rather than go to church or watch television in darkness, might
well be relatives of Froissart, have a rogue trace of his blood in
their veins, be dead ringers of his stony face in the square at
Valenciennes.

There is, of course, no party. La Taverne is the most local of
locals. Nothing is fizzing except marginally the beer. The
oblong of bar overlooks a courtyard with a young chestnut
in no hurry to drop conkers. A dozen chaps, the odd woman,
look as though they are in permanent residence. The beer has a
loud voice. It keeps darkly laughing, with such a rattle of
hilarity that Frédéric, the landlord, goes outdoors to answer his
mobile, while the froth drains down the glasses. It is puncti-
lious of Estinnes to have a tavern named after me, when I was
only the parish priest. I feel obscurely honoured for having
written books. They all look at the stranger out of eyes
discreetly averted as from religion.

A native of Hainault, Froissart was here for years, a *hennuyer*
from top to toe. Home it was, homeland. It is no good my
exploring this place on foot. Only his mind is here, sunk in the
boringness of everything that meets the eye only to repel it. But
he throve on these dull pastures. Every morning he picked up his
pen without a thought or doubt or twinge. I think myself he was
fat. The stomach swelled into self-satisfaction beneath the
clerical garment designed to conceal it. He little knew at this
stage that his portly dimensions would be reproduced in stone

and flaunted in public squares named after him. I imagine the parsonage, that one servant slipping in and out of the shadows, his hand rising under the sackcloth skirt at her buttock as she slops more wine into his glass, a good day's work done, more history pinned down, a king immortalised, a battle fought to the finish.

Time presses me into a mere afternoon for Chimay, yet here Froissart lived out at least two decades of a retirement that was a reinvention of his history. He kept on rebuilding his century, an inveterate reviser, with a burning intent to reach a final truth which half a millennium later will be scorchingly questioned, razed to groundlessness, by the hindsight of academic opinion. Like Estinnes, his parish, Chimay stands on a hill, a relative rarity in the flats of Hainault, an undulation so modest that, like most of the prose of his decriers, it never excites the eye. Both places seem self-contained, the church dominant, the streets as narrow as minds.

Oddly Chimay is as quiet now as then, a murmur of a town. Only the human voice interrupts the calm which almost amounts to a spell. The church's bulk shadows the windows of small dignified houses, behind which even smaller footnotes are being infinitely perfected by clerics. Here Froissart was granted a canonry, just as Machaut was in Reims; a sinecure that defines leisure as without limit.

You breathe middle-class air in the big dark church. Three bays of the chancel Froissart saw and lived with; they were erected in the century before him. I light a candle in the chapel that faintly shines on the letters cut into his plaque in Latin. He spends an eternity ageing on this spot, coming and going, resisting depression, trying to improve his book, feeling lonely, striving to get the past right for the future. Somewhere he is buried.

There is one more call to make for Froissart: the site of the most hopeful treaty of the whole of the Hundred Years War. Not to go is equivalent to never reflecting on irony or never contemplating the tomb of the unknown warrior: big sins. It is at Brétigny, close to Chartres, on the way home. You have to plough through a vast amount of warfare to reach it and cross at speed an uncountable number of bodies unaccounted for, the bones that centuries of politics have left in the earth of these dull swathes of northern France.

Brétigny turns out to be a tiny secretive village off the modest D139 out of Chartres to the east. It can be no larger now than then. It looks lost. A few villas hide behind high hedges of well-cut shrub, a few farms behind high walls of stone. Small, square and enclosed, closed in on itself, the village has four streets, more lanes really, all named from history, all proud and sad.

The Rue du Traité runs along one edge and peters out into open country, off it the Rue Jean le Bon 1360, summarising that moment early in the Hundred Years War when both sides were deluded into thinking the war might be over for good. No less tragic in the aftermath, but more recent, more personal, are the other two street names which commemorate and mourn more sons of the village than could be spared then or ever: the Rue des 3 Frères Girard 1914–1918 and the Rue des 4 Frères Moreau 1914–1918. The war memorial tells me that the Girards were christened Léon, Raymond and Stanislas; the Moreaus were Abel, Charles, Lucien and Paul. I find myself quietened, an intruder, plunged into a silence of useless death in conflict with useful hope, a peace treaty that ends in the trenches, a humane conclusion that matures 500 years later into a contortion of young corpses and old rustic grief. For this place, on its two entries into history, the peace came first, the war later.

A few kids draw back from kicking around a football to stare at the car. There is nobody else in sight, but I feel disinclined to get out. Once in 1360 Brétigny was as self-important as Versailles in 1919 and as vital to history and as hopeless to progress. So many lives depended on it. The world's eyes were upon its wisdom. I need to know it at first hand, not through the blurred window of either a car or anyone else. I must see it and feel it. Froissart was here; I am a reporter. I step out. The car door slams like a gunshot. I lock it. A farmer crossing his yard pauses to gaze at me with gross suspicion.

I stare the place out. Was Froissart actually present at the conference on 1 May 1360? If not, he missed a bevy of thirty-eight ambassadors, English and French, a trio of papal legates, the massed ranks of their bodyguards, servants, messengers, just the class of material for a 23-year-old reporter to cut his teeth on and an incipient snob to suck up to. At a pinch Chaucer too, having been ransomed on 1 March at Reims, might have turned up here. He returned to England two months later, possibly with the fleet that brought the treaty home, embarking at Honfleur on 19 May. In any case it was unlikely that they met.

Brétigny, however, marks the moment when Froissart, no longer needing to sponge off le Bel's history, became his own man. Rarely at first did he put his own personage in the forefront of the narrative. Only later, when noble patrons and even royal approval had persuaded an essentially modest and modern man that he was not without his own tinge of distinction, albeit in letters rather than in battle, did he emerge from anonymity and, with a good line in patter, turn himself into the anchorman of his *Chroniques* as well as quite a showman.

His most openly personal moment came in the autumn of 1388 when Froissart determined at the peak of his career that without first-hand material he would be unable to deal to his satisfaction with a succession of mighty events in Southern Europe. 'And if I should tell that such things happened and not tell openly the whole matter,' he said elsewhere, 'it would be a chronicle but no history.' So he got himself to Carcassonne, whence on horseback over many days, picking up anecdotal company along the way, he journeyed west towards the court at Orthez of Gaston Phoebus, Comte de Foix, a wild old privateer and prince who enjoyed the good life, was writing a book on hunting and with a wily independence ran this area of France parallel to the Pyrenees.

Froissart had got it into his head that Gaston had up his sleeve a trick or two worth knowing. Not only would he beard this dictator in his castle but, to build up the expectation, tell the story in his own words of the trouble he took to reach him in that remote fastness. At last, for the first time, the investigative reporter was turning into the commentator who put his own personality in front of his goods, thus possibly obscuring their value as fact but ensuring their value as fun.

Much in this village is ramshackle, ill-kept outbuildings echoing my sense of Brétigny's hostility, yet dozens of doves brood on the rooflines of barn and villa alike. Soon I make off, marvelling at the smallness of history as shown in places as little as

Brétigny or Compiègne that have meant huge amounts to whole nations, turning my back on peace and principle as the Clio almost on autopilot turns right in the vague direction of Le Havre to make the overnight ferry to Portsmouth.

V AUGUST IN SWEDEN

Back home in England the next part of the plan is to track down
Froissart in the shadow of the Pyrenees, where for some weeks
on the hoof, or rather on horseback, he is to become magnifi-
cently himself.

So I make the plans. Funds are low. I have no patrons. No one is
pitching in with a daily pitcher. It costs nothing to log on to the
website of a budget airline. I tell nobody in our London house of
my intended travel, usually earning scorn for my attempts to locate
the Internet, so I try it late at night. Sure enough, Ryanair whizzes
you once a day to Carcassonne in the time it takes Froissart to cover
10 miles at a trot. I tap in my preferred dates with the gambler's
tension that assails an amateur when he waits for the computer to
crash or the website to fade or the cost to stun.

The system comes up trumps, however: outward journey
£8.99, home for 1p. Only the airport tax, all being relative,
mildly hurts. But the total is still there and back for £33. I reach
for my debit card and enter my details. I am confirmed as being
on next Monday's FR72 flight leaving London Stansted at 10.40
for Carcassonne, returning three days later on FR73 at 14.00. I
feel at once in the midst of things, with a satisfaction that floods
to the tips of the toes.

Clearing the desk, I lay out the spiral-bound Michelin Atlas
Routier (1cm = 2km) at the spread, pages 178–9, which on the
right-hand side just fits in half of Carcassonne, including not only
the airport but the D119 to Montreal which as Montroyal (in the
Lord Berners 1525 translation) was Froissart's first pause. To the
map's side I place the text under the lamp. I can now follow the
journey in a tripartite mixture of the literal (there it stands on the
page), the imaginative (eye passing across the map like a plane
over landscape), and the alteregoistic: I am Froissart, I am myself,
I have forgotten who or what I am in the excitement of plotting
out, from a guide written centuries ago, a journey I am taking
and have yet to take. I can spend hours poring over this pleasure,
and I do. It is a total reality because that country is still there,
strung with hamlets visited by the chronicler on his manic search
for material; and I am flying to it next week, to be alone on low-
cost horsepower moving down lanes as ill paved as the Pilgrim's
Way.

But the present springs yet another lure to put at risk any such
immediate expedition into the past.

An old and close friend, seen rarely because for so long living
abroad, is giving a big party in the south of Sweden to warm his
newly built house. It means cutting off in mid paragraph my
report on Froissart's reporting, for I could hardly take the old
chronicler with me except in book form. But something
intrinsic to the occasion, a shadow not of relief but of promise,
draws me to accept, against the grain of dashing to the fourteenth-century Béarn for £33 (a sum which I now have to
surrender), and I puzzle over the fact at crack of dawn, in the
populous agony of Stansted awaiting a Ryanair flight (not quite
as cheap) to Malmö, that it has to do with my friend being an

out-and-out media man all his life. As a reason for going to
Sweden, this is less a motive than an excuse: meant to sound as if
I were flying on a crusade to convert this slip of a pensioner away
from the media maelstrom to a decent retirement like mine.

The ankle dragged along the unending corridor to the
departure lounge, only to be told to proceed at once and at
speed to a gate half a mile away. On this no-frills airline, reacting
to the prospect of boredom, I had given in to the thin end of the
wedge – newspapers so thick under my arm that in my haste they
kept falling apart. Panic headlines tumbled out of my grip.
Sensations went adrift on the polished floors. The prospect of
a Middle Eastern conflagration slid across several yards to land up
at someone's feet in a coffee concession. In the slipstream of
fellow passengers I limped to the right gate, my wake aflutter
with the gigantic confetti of stories I would never have time to
pick up and read. I took all these exclusives biting the dust as a
lesson without knowing what on earth it taught.

But – what relief on the plane – I had Froissart in my shoulder
bag. He was in three translations, Berners, Johnes and Jolliffe, the
relevant pages photocopied for hand luggage. I also had the map
of where I now ought to be travelling. With two seats I spread
myself. I refused champagne at £7.50 the quarter bottle, 750
times less cheap than the return fare from Carcassonne. Meanwhile Froissart was landing up south, as I flew north.

Beyond the wing we lifted above East Anglian clouds just as
Froissart passed out of Montroyal 'and so to Fanjeaux, then to
Bellepuis and then to the first town of the earl of Foix, and then
to Mazères and so to the castle of Saverdun, and then I came to
the good city of Pamiers', where Froissart, tiring of solitude,

perhaps tired of cataloguing places, 'tarried abiding for some company going into the country of Béarn, where the earl was'. He admitted to all his translators that he liked the town. Berners says he found it 'delectable'. The Victorian Johnes confines himself to the merely 'delightful'. Jolliffe ignores the passage. They all made it hard to focus a clear picture. I am a camera? I was not a camera. Somewhere above Aldeburgh the imagination started to sag. Like Avis, with whom I had booked the hire car in Sweden, I tried harder.

At this pause in Pamiers I felt in the society of these differing translators as I limped up the stairs of an inn or painfully led my horse through the stench of the streets. They kept falling out. A simple word often divided them. They corrected one another in a mannerly but pedantic fashion. I erred on the side of thinking Berners the most sophisticated of the bunch and I pitied his exile in Calais, capital of the booze cruise. I kept foreseeing a quarrel break out between the three centuries that were all dead and gone. But no, they had not vanished. That was a part neither of my thesis nor of my gut feeling: all were as alive as ever at any time human will and mind cared to tune into them.

Meanwhile Froissart and I enjoyed looking at the fine vineyards surrounding Pamiers and sat pondering by the clear broad flow of the Ariège. I waited ensconced in the Hôtel de France on demi-pension looking for scraps of past that might as well be cuneiform for all the help they gave. From the outlines on the map this was not a town secure from boredom, despite the double curve of the river that bracketed it into place. I decided to compress Froissart's three days into an hour of determined research on the plane.

Below the North Sea glittered black. At a zinc counter in

Pamiers, with intent to buy them drinks, I talked to a citizen or two to test local memory. At the name of Froissart they shrank into ignorance, paid their own tab, turned on their heel, gazed unseeingly upwards at a television set gabbling unheard under the ceiling, then scurried towards the delectable tedium of home. Either I had lost my skills as a journalist or in these parts they cared less than a jot about Froissart.

Here on the knees were the xeroxed pages of the Guide Michelin. A quick calculation: it was only 30 miles to St Girons, where Eychenne had one Michelin star, and you could drive the whole of Froissart's daily stint on the road in half an hour. From the specialities I ordered the *foie de canard frais aux raisins*, washed down by Pacherenc du Vic-Bilh, and the *gigot de lotte safrane*, leg of eel-pout being the translation; not unlike Froissart it sounded better in French. This (within red quotes) '*bel amènagement intérieur*' was well off Froissart's route, but never mind. I had grown impatient waiting for him to await a travelling companion. My hired car would catch him up, especially if fuelled with a spot more of that Pacherenc. I drove back from the restaurant into a town tottering on the verge of paradise.

Froissart has absconded. It seemed that at the Hôtel de France he made quick friends with a knight called Espan de Lyon, a handsome fellow of fiftyish, on his way back to Orthez from a spell of offering homage or treachery to the Pope in Avignon. The noble Espan was longing for news of the north of France, the good Jean's home from home, and Froissart in turn ached to impart to a new friend his knowledge of past bloodshed along their way westwards. But first they had to conquer a mountain, Cosse, hundreds of steep feet above the Ariège valley – enough to take your breath away, no good for narrative in the saddle, no

good for bad ankles, good for bonding, 'an evil passage' (Berners), 'difficult of ascent' (Johnes). Sir Espan and his listener were
now locked in mutual respect. Thereafter every castle they
passed released an anecdote or a tragedy, each an illustrious
jape in which those who gained the day were honoured to the
echo if only because those who failed were dead. These two
men, in the stories they swopped, were the media afoot.

Otherwise the flight to Malmö is uneventful. Except for one
thing: in the absence of newspapers in the air I have time to look
into the blue or into that part of the brain that makes things up. It
is not quite as good as the reality of being in the south. Yet, eyes
resting on a featherbed of clouds, coming down to earth, I get a
further inkling of why this visit fits; nothing is random, unless
everything is.

In Sweden four decades ago I, like my host, was spellbound by
the media: broadcasting on Sveriges Radio for weeks on end,
scripting documentaries for the BBC, taping soundtracks on a
primitive recorder as heavy as excess baggage, drafting outlines
for feature films, labouring over screenplays, taking still pictures
on the set during productions, interviewing actresses on their
privacy for the purposes of publicity – yes, earning my living by
putting up a performance in obeisance to the media. But this trip
is not to exorcise years haunted by the temporal. Nor need this
visit spark off any shame over an addiction to daily doses of the
drug of proliferating the unnecessary in word or image.

This journey is to honour a friend.

The first comfort in Sweden is how empty of man the land is
and how loose its grip on time. The road from the unflustered
airport leads at once into open country that feels secret. A sense

of being hounded makes me shiver this hot day. Apart from never knowing well these southerly parts of the kingdom, where accents are as flat as fields, I soon find the gathering outcrops of rock inimical. The birches shift uneasily in an absence of breeze. The outlook has the effect of detaching me from whatever I am.

A pause for lunch in Lund, that tightly built university of calm where the pace is negligible, then the drive eastward through the length of an afternoon in which towns grow progressively smaller and farther apart, until a canal draws you to its exit to the sea at Ronneby on to the huge quays and sidings of a port deserted but for a tatty coaster or two docked as if for ever, and after hours more of driving into ever rockier and more primal country, where the roads thin into dusty tracks, the journey ends towards sunset, moon already huge, at the shack of a villa, the Swedish summer house by the sea, where another media friend from former times has accepted my invitation to let me spend the night.

With this friend too, now ranking high in the film hierarchy in Sweden, I have been long out of touch. He sets up movies with cash from any states in Europe which will work with him in the hope of selling those films, once made, to all sorts of countries further afield. His time is spent in the air or in a group talking in a suite in one of a chain of plush hotels that unite the world in a single menu of luxury. He referees the conflict between art and money. It is not, and has never been, what his mind and heart are right for.

We talk of it, at a slant, the need to survive media. Now, on what he claims to be the last day of summer, sharing the irrational poignancy of having been here illusorily for ever but having to pack up next day, we eat fish grilled in the open

on a wooden verandah that overlooks the tranquillity of an inlet
of the Baltic already in the dusk as real as a loss.

At bedtime I look out at the rapt silence of the moonshine,
puzzled still to feel that I am being drawn back to a self I am
pleased to have left behind: a person even more insubstantial
than any of the three men I seek to enter into – Boccaccio,
Froissart, Chaucer – in whichever order or by whatever means.
That old self of mine, tapping keys to a deadline, snapping stars
for film stills, is just as far away as the three pioneers are in terms
of credence and actuality. Anybody's time, once lost, slips
without a ripple into the pool where eternity hardly stirs the
depths. Well, so it forgivably seems in the light of Sweden on a
late summer night that so resembles a dawn.

In bed, leafing through the translations and peering at the map, I
tried to turn Froissart's journey to Orthez into an exercise of
imagination that offset these travels in actual Sweden.

Along that lonely way, parallel to the colossal line of the
Pyrenees moving westward, existed somewhere the essence of
Jean Froissart. In the pages that covered those circuitous distances
he came up front. If not rash with personal detail, he let his prose
reflect him in the places he observed and the persons he met.
Not quite straight reportage, for the reporter is beginning to be
as important to the narrative as the matter reported, but it set a
trend which, to see fulfilled to the utmost, I had only to open a
newspaper: the reporter overwhelming by force of personality
the material he purported, and was paid, to relay deadpan. He
swallowed what he saw, converted it into nourishment for
himself, then excreted it for the rest of us, in an alimentary
analogy that cast upon the process more aspersions than light.

On the D27 Froissart and Espan de Lyon skirted Artigat, no more than a village, and its castle, no less than a ruin, and ended up dining in an elevated château belonging to the Comte de Foix at Carlat. Dining? Probably when I was lunching; medieval mealtimes were different. Anyway they rode on long enough for Espan to tell Jean a richly nasty tale soaked in blood about how that very castle at Artigat met its doom and why the demon drink brought the townsfolk to their knees. The story took 14 km, so to spend the night they ended up in Montesquieu, where if not worth a detour there must be a hotel, but my Michelin stats contained no reference.

Anyway I need not stay in this 'good inclosed town' (Johnes) when there was Sauveterre-des-Comminges to fall back on. Isolated in a *'beau parc'* (Michelin), the Hostellerie des 7 Molles has just the exclusive silence needed to recover from listening for hours to Sir Espan, as droning as Radio 4 in a motorway jam. As long as I was back at Montesquieu good and early, I would miss nothing of note.

The pair set off at dawn for Palaminy, but to Froissart's mild shrug of annoyance an arch of the wooden bridge over the Garonne had been swept away by floods. On enquiry he blamed heavy rain falling in Catalonia; even the more distant Aragon may have been the culprit – how did anyone know? They had no choice but to drag back for the day to Montesquieu, already a candidate for France's capital of ennui.

And they still had to cross the Garonne. Froissart credited the knight with a local know-how that did the trick, involving 'difficulty and danger' (Johnes), if not 'pain and peril' (Berners). Opposite Cazères, they took a bumpy ride in a boat so small it barely had room for a couple of horses and two men. As if to recover from the adventure, they spent the whole day at Cazères, exchanging data, putting in more groundwork on material later to be developed by Froissart for mass consumption.

There was never any hurry then. This century withdrew from pace as it shrank from the plague. While servants were 'preparing their supper' (Johnes) and 'in the mean time that our supper was a dressing' (Berners), Sir John and Sir Espan explored the town, and I walked with them in the recollection of strolling to the heart of dozens of small French towns in the aperitif of twilight. As they reached a town gate, Sir Espan pointed to a breach in the wall recently made good. A story crossed his mind. As Froissart gave ear to it, he could see with his own eyes desperate men creeping through the hole to satisfy hunger as much as to gain freedom from siege. Again it was a drama of this district that spotlighted Gaston Phoebus for his humanity. The historian retold it much moved. The two men ambled back to their lodgings to find supper ready.

My head nodded over the map, on which the distance between my eyes was measured at 25 km, a day's journey.

Next day, as they followed the Garonne, Sir Espan pointed out on the opposite bank castles for whose history he could personally vouch. He was just Froissart's man, a miracle of informative garrulity. 'Sir John, I have witnessed here many excellent skirmishes and combats': thus Johnes had him prefacing a tale in which many died and a castle was razed to its present ruin by hundreds of peasants setting fire to faggots cut from hedges, whereas Berners preferred 'I have seen here many fair scrimmishes and encounterings', while in his turn Froissart made a mental note of a meadow that Johnes found 'beautiful' and

Berners 'fair'. I start to nod off with that tapestry of a field in mind. It had the look of a dream.

I awake briefly staring at the giant moon in the north. The three translators have slithered off the counterpane; the map has shrunk into a squeezebox. What am I up to? It's not that I am too tightfisted to afford yet another fare to Carcassonne, the cost of meals or notebooks or accidents, the possible need for surgery on my ankle, etc. It is more that by the chosen trio of media pioneers – Chaucer, now Froissart, Boccaccio to come – I am being confirmed in the view that most good human things take place in the imagination, fed by fact during the day, then coming out in dreams at night, etc. Etc.

We were our own narrators. Living was a way of telling ourselves the story of our own lives. Living was a way of exercising the inner mind, without the continuously extending use of which we not only might as well die, but did die. We died young, years before our funeral. We died middle-aged of heart trouble, when the doctor said there was nothing wrong with us. We died old from being fatigued by not knowing what it was all about. In this process the last thing we needed was help from the media, though a shout now and then across the chasm of human misunderstanding, in somebody's play, in a book on my knee, or from a busker staring you in the eye, never came amiss: one touch of nature making the world not just kin but calm and collusive, happy even.

This Baltic half-night dissolving into sunshine sharpens the pain of leaving the here and now. The morning quickly clouds. A glance in Kalmar at the castle, girt by parks that embalm it in the Middle Ages, and then in a drizzle across the bridge to the slightly offshore island of Öland known of old, meeting when young on a night that never got dark a publicity girl in tourism who later became a newscaster: yet more of the media echoing back to jog my conscience. The memory all but gone, I see the all-night light, her body velveted by the indifferent gloss of late and early sun.

Öland lies even further in the past than remembered. Spitting rain starts on Alvaret, an upland plateau where the wild flowers thrust out of scrub as dotted as a tapestry viewed by Froissart. Hoping to roam it, I am driven back by squalls into the car, staring out at heath, eating a picnic hand to mouth. There is the sense, even the fear, of being kept from something. Setting a brave face against a resistance stronger than the weather and unidentified, I drive on.

By a burial ground, stones rooted in tussocks of dead grass, the rain now falls in earnest. Only the car just about exists un-washed-out. Down a half-made lane on the edge of the Baltic lies a fishing hamlet with a tiny harbour and a couple of blown boats. Notices long out of date on a board are protected by glass blinded by rain, the words as smudged as runes. A reek of centuries of fish breezes in and out of the air. The sea is as grey as the sky which is as dark as the earth. Other centuries stare me out across blank seas too drenched to offer a horizon, far beyond which lie the tundra, the steppes, the Trans-Siberian railway, the end of the line, the world's terminus.

I know just where I shall finish up. On the map, in Gothic print, a site, still striking me as non-existent or hard of approach: Eketorp. Then, almost past it, a blur of walled town on the skyline inland, at first as misty an image as the waves out to sea, but clearing over the shoulder as the car backs 50 yards into the rain, and there is the hidden turn at first missed. The roads wind so as to keep making it vanish, only to reset it at another angle. But then arrives, windblown and wet, a car park out here in the wild, a few cars drawn up, looking like shelter and solidarity.

Eketorp is a castle, a town, a city, a metropolis. It appears at a remove, not wholly real, through the rapid wipers. The wind blurs it. Vacancy looms. The walled settlement, if restored, has stood here in good shape for over a thousand years. Limping into the cold of the past is scary, yet this is where suddenly with a shiver the past is happening, at the closing of a road that tumbles into the sea. By now, so long cramped by weather and inactivity into the car, I feel unwell and fearful. Not only is the ankle cursing, the feet are giving way to paralysis; eyes blinking behind glasses blinded by rain are beyond assessing the yards it needs to walk to reach the walls. I am in no shape to mount an attack on the mystery.

The walls are blank, but I expect hostility, hundreds of years of it bottled up inside the castle, bursting to unleash on me the barbarism of history. I have no right of entry, my passport irrecoverably in the car, mac soaked and leaking, stick no defence. Though I seem to be getting no nearer, the walls start to rise, then to tower, then to overwhelm, silent in their assertion of defensive violence in the rain. At every slit watches a wary eye. The body shrinks under the combining seep of rain and heat of sweat. It is with all my few resources, facing the challenge of an unplumbable antiquity, that I reach a gate massively fortified only by a woman seated in a box.

She takes my money, hands me a ticket, lets me plunge, cold and wet, into the fortress. The interior is open to the sky, but a pattern emerges of squat long buildings hunched under roofs where for generation upon generation I am allowed to live and eat and sleep and escape rain if not threat. I nip into one of them in search of comfort, shaking myself, and find my typical food laid out in showcases, with simple instructions on how to harvest and cook it, displaying the crude bowl out of which I consume it, using the fingers that are my cutlery. I understand that I shall be living here unchanged for centuries, my annual routine altered only when an invader from afar looses a shower of arrows into our midst, besieges us, starves us out, climbs or batters or blows up our walls in the endless rain, and all at once I am dead.

Only to be resurrected into the cold and pain and wet of engineering this return to roots miles further back in time than my own – an effort to void my mind of knowledge and leave it open to ignorance, superstition, fear; to regain the innocence of thinking that all I need know of life I can find out for myself without being told. Information will only flummox my brain. The opinions of others will sap it of strength. It must fly free.

Now I see why I was drawn again to this inhospitable north. I had forgotten how much older the north was, and how in my thirties in Sweden I had been intimidated by its glacial secrecy and frightened by its vast indifference, and how in my seventies I can now expand into age and space. No wonder now I think I can be Chaucer, or Froissart for that matter, not to mention Boccaccio.

As yet none of them is born. From where I stand in the downpour, they are the future. So I am relieved of time. Or, more modestly, I am freed of the media by a simple act of deciding they have yet to happen. Or, more imaginatively, my heart and mind are released back into a modern world where only a private sense of adventure can determine what I care to make of life.

My old friend's house-warming passes off in a haze of pleasure. His hospitality is rich enough to rival the staying power of an average medieval feast. I see him faintly as a doppelgänger of mine, still doing what we both used to do, earning his keep from communication. Throughout the party, which lasts a couple of days, I find I am looking at him as a past self, someone outgrown, all the more admirable for not having thrown broadcasting out of his life, not given up writing for the papers, not caved in to my fears: holding fast to what is best in him. Meanwhile I persist in being glad of this chance to get off my fingers the ink – as well as the cacophony out of my ears, the taste out of my mouth, the sights out of my sore eyes, the stench out of my nostrils – of the daily assault by the media on what little virtue I have left.

The flight home from Malmö Sturup is delayed enough to drink aquavit and eat prawns amid the late-night echoes of an empty airport. From Stansted the drive home to Kent seems short in the small hours, though by now I am keen to catch up with Froissart. In the garden a pathetic whimper disturbs the air as of an animal in pain: the burglar alarm at a last gasp of warning as its battery runs out of juice. In my absence the electricity has been cut off.

Striking matches at intervals I search blindly for candles, the wicks chewed down by mice looking for traps with cheese on. In the freezer the peas are soggy, partridges soft of breast, ice cubes converted into tepid water. In gross anxiety, as if life will never improve, my spirit whizzes back to the fourteenth century, lost for ever in its long night, awaiting a dawn that will never break except to further stress.

It breaks sleeplessly. With anxiety, too early, I haunt our neighbours' front door, only for it to be flung open: all goodwill as usual, hot tea, toast, the telephone, invitation to lunch. Enough relief floods in to make me almost glad the night happened as it did. The emergency man turns up at noon to pinpoint the cause of chaos as a fault in the cooker that tripped the system that alerted the alarm, a set of facts that for another instant within a day or two, a thousand miles apart, has left me alone in the Middle Ages, having to face the wet centuries of Eketorp under constant threat or just a gathering corruption in the fridge, the stink to live with, the cold water to wash in, the alienation produced by a shock of discomfort suddenly imposed by a failure of the modern.

However far I choose (or am able) to move next, I now have a foretaste of what it is like. If I had not gone the distance to Eketorp, my own home in Kent would not have let me down. If I had not attended my friend in his warm house amid the forests, a particular chill of the past would have been denied me. All day, slowly recovering nerve, I know that by accident or will or chance or desire I have got myself detached from living a normal life in the dead centre of today. I am separated from time. From habit I go to the village shop, but all but the sex tabloids have sold out. The rest of the village is being eaten up by the sensational present I have almost sidestepped. I am hanging on to it only by the fingertips, wondering when and where I will drop.

The easier option, asap, is to make further arrangements to go back to France and Froissart.

★   ★   ★

The moment I tried imagining his journey to Orthez from the page, I had a strong urge to go and prove myself right or wrong or just misguided.

So I am back on the Internet, making at greater cost a budget booking as last week to Carcassonne. I memorise the reference (H91ADT) which is my only passport to the air above Stansted, apart from my passport. Vests are ironed, shirts folded, trousers dry-cleaned, sunglasses sought, socks washed, euros bought, bags packed. I travel armed with the usual loose sheets of badly copied pages of books plus, as a makeweight designed to pull my shoulder out of its socket at airports, a copy of *The Hunting Book of Gaston Phoebus*, a wonder of wonders, a true treat. At least I have managed not to take on the journey two pairs of greyhounds and a saddlebag stuffed with parchment.

To be obvious about it, France is always a surprise when you stray from the obvious. Once away from the impressive falsity of the old city of Carcassonne, put on the map by Viollet-Le-Duc and Prosper Mérimée – the Middle Ages writ risible – the tract of country Froissart chose to cross is little different today. His route is plainly traceable over the hills, even where he is less than precise in reference. The only signs of life are those not of poverty but of depopulation, ruined farms, swathes of meadow tapestried with such a wealth in flowers as no modern agriculture would allow.

Most of the paths he took are on straight and level upland lanes, on which you meet no traffic, with views of huge extent on either side, often magnificent: the Pyrenees rise to the south in an unfolding vision of a grandeur that mounts ever higher into unseeable distance. Does he notice all this? How do rural aesthetics strike the medieval mind? Look at Piers Plowman,

at Chaucer too, for the odd sign of an attitude to landscape: what
we live in and on, after all, with our fellow creatures, lying
somewhere between the frightening and the domestic and the
beautiful and the cruel, the ground our grave, the sky our hope.
But it is better to occupy the high ground, for no moral reason,
just to avoid bandits.

I skip at speed the places I have imagined Froissart in, especially
the 'delectable' (Berners) Pamiers, now regarded as 'a disappoint-
ment' (*Rough Guide*), a fan of outlying avenues lined with garages
and supermarkets centring on a few decrepit towers. I also almost
give a miss to Cazères, where he lost his nerve crossing the
Garonne on a dicey vessel, never recording how he coped on
the turbulent brown water (if like today) with the two pairs of
greyhounds, his poetic tribute to Gaston, or how he kept his
parchment dry. The place is still a centre of *batellerie* or lighterage,
the carriage of goods by boat. To distract him from the dangers, Sir
Espan is saying, 'Sir John, let us go and see the town,' so I obey,
adding it to a private list of French towns in which it would be
agreeably easy to sink into anonymity or escape a crime.

A Michelin guide I buy in a *tabac* tells me that pilgrims and
merchants rested here on their way from Toulouse and points
north before an arduous crossing of the Pyrenees. The local
history, much as expounded by Sir Espan on his peregrination
with Sir Jean, lies among documents preserved in the fourteenth-century church. A scholar might spend months amid that
trésor, as Michelin terms it, looking for a sample of Froissart's
handwriting, a scrap that flew out of his hand when crossing the
Garonne and landed high and dry. The calm of the place makes
you think that there could be worse fates for a winter than
digging for it in the archives.

The track moves westward in line with the mountains. At a pause, a roadside picnic above a river, a modern book about him says that he 'depicts himself as possessed by the need to travel and find out'. That touch renders him at once human, a small boy grown up. Thus a venture, undertaken at some risk, became adventure. His triple desire is to persuade his visits abroad to tell him the truth, then to pass on the whole truth to a wider world, then to be lauded for his skills in formulating nothing but the truth.

But the truth is darkly otherwise. Not for nothing is he cast as a founding father of the media. 'By 1388 he was aware that he is the author of a work that will be read by posterity,' says a French authority in 1953. This gives him the right not only to ask questions as ever, but to translate the answers into his own idiom, to edit those answers, buff up their style, so that in the end even poor old Sir Espan is talking with many a literary grace note in Froissart's tone of voice; the rough diamond picked up by the roadside in Pamiers has been polished into the glitter expected of a workshop in Chimay, where Froissart later retires to perfect his notes and recite them, altering them for the better as mood dictates, to a dozen scribes.

The picnic is over. On this trip Froissart's methods have undergone a shift. Putting himself to the fore, the old reporter is making over his material and telling us directly what he thinks of it. He is his own impresario, a compère to history's gigs, a personality standing with some authority in the way of viewing things as they really are, and for the life of me, as I stuff the picnic's remnants into paper bags, I cannot help thinking: good old Froissart, you've hit your stride.

Meanwhile on the outskirts of Orthez he trots in triumph

alongside the four lanes of the future A64. He has arrived at the promised land. He is not only at the peak of his profession, but on holiday at someone else's expense. Fame has freed him of the anonymity that stiffens the manner of the first books of (his spelling) *croniques*. He is entering (ditto) *istoire*.

Illusorily strengthened by a pastis in the Café Place des Armes, the ankle lets me hobble down the steep cobblestones of the Rue Bourg Vieux to a river that is as wide a sweep of the immemorial as you can expect at one gulp. The water roars down under the Pont Vieux (everything is old here), with a watchtower just off centre, built by an ancestor of Gaston when he made Orthez capital of the Béarn. On the other bank stone steps run down to the barques no longer tied up for quick commerce or escape.

In serenity I sit awkwardly on rocks above the river's loud silence. Froissart is in Orthez for at least three months, so this is his stroll, his rest, when duty proves too much at the château (except it never does) and he is expected to read his poems late into the night (except he loves it). But this town is still Gaston's; it feels primally medieval, however patched up. The street plan is his. Quirks of decoration at the corners of houses survive, so do windows that have evaded the vandalism of fashion or bad builders. A church once defending the north wall has arrow slits where any believer might expect stained glass. And uphill the narrowing perspective, a dizzying wriggle of streets, strains towards the high keep, the Tour Moncade, which kept Gaston Phoebus secure and his media-minded guest well entertained. In the ascent the ankle gets flustered, so I take the hired car up, parking it at the angle of a cannon aimed at Gaston's defences.

It is municipal gardens now, this castle. In the shop on the ground floor of the keep you can buy for a few euros a bottle of an aperitif called Hypocras invented by Gaston. On the west side of that keep you can view the circumflex outline of the pitched roof of the hall, now only a lawn, where he nightly put his hospitality at Froissart's disposal. At once Gaston struck our reporter as of odd habits. 'Que il se couchoit et levoit à haute nonne,' he observed of his host's regimen of rising at noon and supping at midnight. 'Our acquaintance was strengthened by my having brought with me a book,' translates Johnes in the 1850s, 'containing all the songs, ballads, rondeaux and virelays,' Berners continues in the 1550s, 'which by imagination I had gathered together.' From these ample pages of his romance *Meliador*, packed to the illuminated margins with derring-do, Froissart was invited to read aloud after supper; 'there was none durst speak any word,' claims the Berners version, 'because he would I should be well understanded.' The copy, no doubt richly embellished, which Froissart presents to the Comte de Foix as a humble tribute, is politely returned to its author at the end of his stay. However riveting the material, one ritual reading a night for twelve uninterruptible weeks smacks of excess. If Froissart does little by halves, he has not half met his match in the autocratic Gaston.

But by now I know I have reached him: he is so happy here in Orthez, as am I, loving the end of a journey, the climax of a search, the leisure that looms thereafter. He and I relish every moment of playing honoured guest to the man he at once realises to be his all-time hero and I see simply as a celeb with no trace of a desire to sidestep the limelight that Froissart's fame as a chronicler might catch him in. Pouring too the syrup of flattery on to this 59-year-old of many parts, in a flash writing off 'all the

very many knights, kings, princes and others' he has met,
Froissart 'never saw none like him of personage, nor of so fair
form nor so well made'. He speaks lingeringly of 'his visage fair,
sanguine and smiling, his eyen gray and amorous'. He goes too
far. Only a few years the Comte's junior, he seems in the act of
falling in love with the fellow.

Rarely has an interviewer given utterance to the free flow of
his feelings with such sincerity – until now when everyone with
such insincerity does it on chatshows, often with intent to take
the hero down a notch or vaunt a futile fame. In these passages
Jean Froissart comes into himself, and you are in the presence,
even as I stand here on the sward above which once spread the
overarching roof of the hall, of a man consumed by enthusiasm,
savouring the quirks of character in others, respecting honour as
sharply as he enjoys privilege, savouring the south at Orthez with
as keen an appetite as he looks forward to transporting all his
scribbled parchment back to his northern privacy at Chimay, to
revise it, improve it, give it to the world: a first journalist, an
ever-eager prototype (but never hiding the warmth under the
chill of cynicism) of the men who gathered at El Vino in the
Fleet Street of my hack youth, who somehow mislaid their lives,
and those of the people they reported, in a mixture of drink and
dryness, in the cause not of the deeper search but of the wider
entertainment.

All right, Froissart can be viewed as the source of the printed
untruth, the lie that dares not edit out its name. But I take his side
with as much affection, and wonder, as he took Gaston's, if only
for the sense that he invested his all in his observation and gave
his all in expressing it. Here at Orthez I reach his summit with
him; know what the ideals are; wonder if I can live up to them –

meanwhile content for two hours to listen to Gaston's midnight feasts, where twelve servants place a lighted torch before their master, and he heartily eats poultry, but only the wings and thighs, after an all-day abstinence, and they converse, as Johnes renders it, 'on arms and amours'.

VI AUTUMN IN TUSCANY

For once life plays into my hands. Wondering where to stay in Florence, in an effort to bring Boccaccio back home, more journalism being no option, out of the blue comes an invitation to apply for a writer's residency. No more than 20 miles south-east of Florence, this act of grace will unbelievably put a four-teenth-century signal tower at my disposal. I shall be waving flags or lighting bonfires.

At first the idea of going to Santa Maddalena seems a cop-out. The nature of my research resists being subsidised, I stand on my own two feet or expire, I must not be bought. Yet a bit of luck can at a pinch be made to look as if Boccaccio is personally inviting me, perceiving my need of help and hospitality. I apply by return of post. As instantly as email, in fact by fax, not Giovanni Boccaccio but the Baroness Beatrice Monti della Corte von Rezzori invites me to stay in her Tuscan home for six weeks. With a bounding heart I envisage her at once as my Fiammetta. She too is in her seventies, and I am in a seventh heaven.

In a dither of excitement and fear between London and Kent in the run-up to departure, I gather my resources like Froissart on his haul to Orthez, or Chaucer preparing for a mission to

Italy. At the canonry in Chimay I dig into a creaky drawer to make sure my passport is in date. In the rooms over Aldgate I pat my pocket to feel the specie bulging within. I assemble my orders, I pack my books, with my finger I spell out on a map the trend of the journey. With a light heart, a heart also in my boots, I say goodbye to wife and children. I am having the trecento dropped in my lap.

No obvious route is to be taken, no motorway. Small roads will slow the car down to no more than a few times the speed of Froissart trotting south. Nobody must guess the purpose: which is to be taken aback by events of my choosing or making without being noticed or reported. It seems a good recipe for living, indeed for staying alive. Halt at nightfall, keep the mind free of any irrelevancy happening in the world at large; switching on the radio for traffic news only as a last resort. Take your time as if time really did belong to you.

I sit in the queue for the ferry with a huge sense of occasion. Even I cannot think the trip matches in scope or bravado the search for the North-West Passage, the race to the South Pole, the landfall on the eastern tip of Vinland. But I make no secret (to myself) of thinking my journey more vital. I am all I have for sure; there is an inner world to be won out there.

Three days and nights of dropping southwards into time lie ahead. Without a word of his language I will be left grounded in the forbidding presence of Boccaccio, about whom I know nothing except as an amalgam of overt pornographer and covert depressive, and this only from books often less reliable than hearsay. I picture him looking as squat and glum as Mussolini. My prejudice for or against Italians springs from a childhood in which they kept running away in jackboots or being strung up by the heels. Any amount of the genius of centuries past – Leonardo, Raphael, Manzoni, Svevo, Silone, Fellini – has to work hard to blot out a boy's war fought out in the daily rags and mags of the 1940s. Thus subjective is history as first reported in newspapers. A good story makes history as petty as the eyewitness wants it to be. One point of the trip is to grow less tiny.

Actually I know a bit more about Boccaccio than I pretend. His home town of Florence is his disliked metropolis. Nonetheless he never goes too far from home, except on paper. As a diplomat he travels west to Avignon which the plan is to bypass and briefly into the Tyrol which is off the northern edge of the chosen route. To the south, beyond the reach of my millimetre-to-the-mile, his range takes him early to Naples, where much of his youth is spent straining to follow in his father's footsteps as a banker.

In that hot-tempered city, where the ruler is Angevin, the language favoured by society is French. The young Boccaccio considers wasted the six years of a discipline in commerce, an echo of Chaucer's seven lost years, but his stories are later to be packed with the detail his eye caught of life at court, in the rough of trade, on the tumble of the quayside.

Only thirteen when he arrived, twenty-seven on leaving, in those later years at Naples he grows into himself. Having with the old man's permission exchanged commerce for the law, he reads widely rather than studies deeply. At home he entertains in style the bloods of an aristocracy more sophisticated than anyone in upstart Florence, his manners honed by mingling with men of letters, for whose art and craft Naples in these days is a brilliant focus.

So Giovanni starts to write, he writes verse, he writes rhymed verse in reams, as well as prose, endless prose, page upon page of the prosaic, and all of it about love, medieval romance falling over itself to be derivative; and in the excitement of it all, longing never to have to read a word of it all, I wonder if I might have time left over on this trip to follow him south into the exuberance of Naples, where my memory throws up only the rowdiness of a fish restaurant at a dock, hasty streets at every turn threatening accident, looking over my shoulder for shadows of the mafia.

Behind me on the ferry the chalk of the Dover cliffs has the look of a great white hope facing an invisible France. Europe is the ghost of an idea in the offing. The boats I see out to sea are bobbing in my childish bath, the gulls are chattering in and out of the eaves above the nursery I never had. By now I am well over halfway between the nothing much behind me and the vast ahead.

A tangent from Calais leads into territory familiar to Froissart. His home town of Valenciennes is only 30 miles to the east. Somewhere near St Quentin the 1914–18 battlefields gather over the mind with the effect of a thunderstorm never off the horizon. The cared-for cemeteries unfold in a tragedy still not played out. In mood much of this land remains as devastated by Edward III in his half-century of fighting for it, as by the Great War more than half a millennium later. Its spirit lies eternally interred.

Next morning, as usual on the first day away from home, the mind salivates for a picnic. The car swings down towards Alsace close to numbers of other battles binding together the ages. To

the left Verdun passes unobserved, not unremembered, the lump
of France's freefall into abject heroism still sticking in my throat.
A mile or two off to the west of that gargantuan sacrifice is, as
usual, a small town with a market.

The journey from now on has to go deeper. Even as I slip
into the cool box the greaseproof complement of ham and
cheese, the flourish of radishes, the bread and wine, I wonder
whether I am here in unknown places because I want to do a
runner from my own life: not just being imposed on, blanked
out, by the media, but failing to keep up, overcome age,
break ground. Perhaps the only honourable way to resist age
is to go back to beginnings; perhaps a mind as it starts to fade
grows younger. All the arguments end up as runny as the
cheese.

I want to picnic beside the Rhine. The river's spread and
power are a medieval thoroughfare too good to miss. So is its
frontier symbolism. But as I skirt Strasbourg industrial complexes
block the river off. Suburbs crowd it out. Long sweeps of bypass
glimpse no water and sliproads promise lanes that lead only to
dead ends of marsh that might or might not have riverside
beyond. It is as if the great arteries of Europe are furred by the fat
of overdevelopment. In the end it takes an hour to gain access to
the Rhine and then only by chance. Raw ham is munched while
looking over at Germany. It turns out to be a long moustache of
trees fringing a thin lip of horizon.

I looked ahead to a particular event: attending that great,
unobtrusive, unwitting, festive – historically unsound, of course
– meeting of my three pioneers in 1368 at the wedding in Milan
of Lionel, Duke of Clarence. The few facts were so far between

that anyone with half an eye was at liberty to invent, as a tabloid
reporter might but with an impulse so different that it hurt, the
facts, the real facts, and nothing but the fiction that improved the
facts. Yet no act of the imagination took flight without a dash of
probability.

I doubted whether Chaucer and Froissart, though on the road
at roughly the same time, were taking this route. In those days
one way to Italy certainly involved crossing the Alps, but
Froissart was more likely to stick to France for as long as possible,
barging down the Rhône, crossing Provence on horseback,
avoiding the heights. As for Chaucer, I had no image of him
except as a benign presence, a presence of subtler sophistication
than mine, with whom these last stages of the journey were
nervously poised to catch up.

In those days it was only travel, by messengers, that brought
the news. These very roads were deeply rutted, blinding you
with dust in summer, sliding you through the mud of winter,
with every chance that your chosen highway would fail to
connect with a bridge or peter out in dense forest. Edward III
had a dozen or so couriers in constant readiness, Philip of France
as many as a hundred, while lords and prelates made do with two
or three. An unhurried day on horseback might manage 40
miles, so that the morning's hot news in Westminster would
reach Hatfield or Haslemere by drinks time; multiply by two for
a messenger on foot. With no luggage, travelling light, with a
regular change of horse, a hundred miles a day (and night)
brought the good news from Bruges to Venice in just a week.
London to Lyons cost the courier 18 days, even if he was lucky in
crossing the Channel, which could require a wait of anything
from three days to a month. You also allowed a month with a

horse for a pilgrimage or even a pouch of documents to reach
Rome from Canterbury.

Night halted all but the most urgent of communications. As of
right a nobleman expected shelter and hospitality in a stranger's
castle or at worst in a monastery. Pilgrims were entitled to a
single free night in the monastery's guest house, never more,
whereas merchants were herded two to a bed into flyblown,
flea-ridden inns packed to the doors with riff-raff and brigan-
dage. On their separate journeys to Florence both Froissart and
Chaucer will have enjoyed a better class of welcome. But were
they actually apart? History suspects that they attended Lionel on
his progress south.

Meanwhile I wondered how the promised signal tower at
Santa Maddalena had actually worked as a means of communication. Time, or timelessness, would tell.

Switzerland in the rain next day puts me in mind of all the ways
of improving myself that I least like. The country itself unfolds as
abysmally as a lecture: the auditoria of the mountains ringed in
mists of dullness, the lakes as flat as texts, the rain making its point
in an unending sermon. The radio either nags me with facts I
need not know or throbs me to sleep with pastime pop; they
have found a way of making radio speak in the long tunnels that
shortcut the mountains. Even in the earth's depths, with millions
of tons only just not bearing down on your skull, but lorries
bearing down on you with headlamps boring into your eyes,
you cannot elude the voice spitting advice at you or the modish
musak treacling into your ear. Accompanied by the media, the
tunnels through the Alps are a waking nightmare devised by
man, arousing the myths that terrorised childhood, the descent

to Hades, the journey to the centre of the earth; being buried alive while reading Edgar Allen Poe. This longest tunnel takes more than a day on horseback and days on foot. I put both Chaucer and Froissart through the experience on their way to Milan and they expire from shock long before they reach the open air.

Happily at the end of the tunnel there is light. The car sweeps out into views far below us of an Italy that massages the eyes with relief and sends the brain tumbling into vertigo.

Next morning, and it seems to take all day, I bypass Milan striving at every sliproad not to be drawn into its whirlpool.

To this city in June 1368 comes Lionel, Duke of Clarence, Edward III's second son after the Black Prince, to marry Violante Visconti, whose name thrills with sexual overtones; she is thirteen. He launches a grand progress towards his second wedding – he was a widower of twenty-nine – at Paris in the spring. For company he has asked along 457 friends, relatives, courtiers, and for some reason, perhaps to distribute them as bounty to landowners or tribute to lords as his train passes through their territory, 1,280 horses.

First he stays at the Louvre in rooms revamped to honour him; the peace woven at Brétigny still not quite threadbare, the French want to add a few strands of luxury to flatter their old enemy, in the apartments that are later to be the setting for the *Mona Lisa*, whose smile is all charm or reverence or scorn, an immortal comment on mortal pretension or courage or folly; had she been painted by then, she would be looking down on Lionel. As many decorations as banquets are heaped on the incipient bridegroom, every Paris street is in a fever of mercantile rivalry for the honour of his custom, Guillaume de Machaut lurks on the margins presenting romances to the rich and noble at a price – yet another chance for our two media men to meet the composer who rings in their ears.

Chaucer travels with the team. So indeed does Froissart. Neither has yet written a word, unless secretly. Both are in Lionel's service. It is no use looking for them in today's Milan, no longer worth thinking of hints or remains; they are better off in the livelier milieu of the mind. If any of the 6,000 drinking fountains remain it can be only an oversight; electricity has long superseded the 300 public ovens, though nowadays more than the fourteenth century's ten hospitals (patients sharing a bed) serve modern needs and a great deal more than the 1,500 lawyers, though a lot fewer than the 10,000 monks, are still in business to look after the other diseases, both temporal and spiritual, of the citizens. Under Visconti's rule the city's walls are maintained by taxing the tarts, who in number may well exceed the combined total of fountains and monks.

Lionel, with Chaucer and Froissart attendant, is greeted at the gates by a guard of honour 1,500 strong borrowed from the Pope, 80 ladies in uniform gowns of gold, scarlet, white, 60 identical knights on horseback. Apart from the dowry, Galeazzo Visconti is paying his son-in-law Lionel's retinue expenses for almost half a year.

On and on goes the autostrada round Milan, a last-ditch attempt to drive round death, to avoid it by risk and ring road, to hope to outdistance it by putting your foot down. Any thought worth the name escapes into a slipstream of spray confusing the windscreens of the cars at your back. Your feelings are so concentrated on surviving that you have no room for real ones.

But at the back of my mind is the nuptial banquet within Milan. It takes place out of doors in high summer. Nobody can quite digest its munificence. Not only are thirty courses of both meat and fish served, crabs setting off the suckling pigs, pike cutting the hare, trout chasing the partridges, a beef pie vying with an eel one, but each dish is gilded with a smearing of saffron, powdered yolk and gold leaf. To allow the guests time to recover between each excess, the whole of Lionel's retinue in due order is given presents. To take random examples of the ranking, I the soldier get a coat of mail, you the count get a begemmed surcoat, he the minor royalty gets a falcon with a silver bell round its neck. Among other gifts, I like to think of Chaucer receiving one of the 'enamelled bottles of the choicest wine' or 'a little palfrey caparisoned in green velvet', both later to come in handy on the pilgrimage to Canterbury, and of Froissart who not at all probably, but desirably, ends up with the grey-hounds in velvet collars, the offspring of which he is later to offload on Gaston de Foix as a pair of compliments. A cloak trimmed with ermine and pearls might go to Petrarch, also present, dining at the top table. Evidence suggests that the old poet and the two novices are unlikely to have exchanged a word, let alone a comradely tip or boast about their respective gifts or (from the sexagenarian sonneteer) some magisterial advice on how to write.

Anyway, they are too busy eating. They are only halfway through the capons with sturgeon when the veal and carp in lemon sauce is served to be closely followed by the meat galantines with lamprey, not to mention the peacocks with cabbage; everything glitters with what really is gold. It takes only four months for Lionel to die: poisoned, people whisper, but death is more likely caused by the gilded food consumed in the massive heat of summer in the valley of the Po. The pubescent bride Violante follows him a while later, thrice a widow at the age of thirty-one.

That July, a month on, Boccaccio is visiting Petrarch a few leagues away in Padua. But has he too, in his last decade a diplomat of note who has used his postings as background for a number of *The Decameron* stories, attended the wedding in Milan? He is already a celebrity in authorship. It is likely that Chaucer looked upon his face, if sidelong. He is later to steal an idea or two from Boccaccio to incorporate in *The Canterbury Tales*. On the banquet's sidelines Froissart eyes him as a possible source of Florentine history he can tap if need be; his ambitions are already on the rise. Even here, where only one of the trio is a proven and published writer, the media are under way.

Because the vernacular is being used, *The Decameron* is already almost twenty years old. It is now respectable to talk rotten, if not dirty. Dead languages are being swept under the literary carpet – Latin is only for the law, Greek for holy writ, both as dry as fluff. A linguistic democracy is in the melting pot and will soon be pouring out its unrefined gold all over Europe, setting in train the whole process that leads to this triumphal minute of having not a single newspaper in the car, wishing to be anywhere but in the car, and devoutly listening to nothing on the car radio. This point in my life, this roar of withdrawal, starts at exactly that moment when on the page the ordinary medievals are reading the same words as people are talking in kitchens or shouting at each other across fields or using for quarrels or firing rounds of verse at the skies.

Chaucer, Froissart, Boccaccio, they must have met, even if,

like the good silent figures that writers best are, they ignored one
another or were too ignorant to make the connections; preferred
to keep their own counsel until ready to speak, and while asking
polite questions of knights and squires at the far extremities of
the banquet, tried the beans and pickled ox-tail or found room
for the junkets and cheese, all the time tongue in cheek.

Out go the pedants on their arses; in come the men with an
ear for their time.

In due course, in and out of storms on the autostrada, I encircle
Florence and head south along the Arno. Down an ever-
narrowing valley river, rail, road run in interlocking parallel
past a war cemetery that unfolds to the water's edge. Numbers of
the East Kents were killed here advancing north to free Florence
of the Germans in 1944.

The Baronessa's directions are clear but coded. She never
indicates that the path into her version of the past leaves a swathe
of modernity behind with every crisp instruction on the fax.
Once off the main road to Arezzo, hairpin bends climb danger-
ously out of the valley's heat. Towards the heights of Vallom-
brosa there are nordic smudges of forest that look coldly dense.
Vineyards switchback in tandem with olive groves; classical
perspectives are revealed, as in the beginnings of Renaissance
art. You plunge into a sudden village, Donnini, of high tawny
houses casting a black geometry of shadow, into a triangular
square with a bar as deep as a crypt, old men embedded in
memory on rickety chairs with the air of extras in post-war
cinema; and then through it you go, on to an even more minor
road that rambles up and down the small hills between places of
habitation or worship that have no windows visible.

Twin pillars are mentioned on the fax. They are rightly said
not to support a gate. Off tarmac on to dust, a decrepit farm, lines
of laundry breezing out like photography typifying the poverty
of Italian life, then at a smallholding a dozen hens squawk at the
windscreen and race at a crouch into dignity: peasant platitude.
The lane runs out of signs of life. A kilometre passes, the trees
thicken, plump yellow cows raise their slow heads from thickets
of fern, the prospect grows more original by the moment, and a
descent begins with a suggestion of stone villa wrapped in
thickets of bamboo posed over vast views. Car doors shut at
a click, oaken doors open at a knock, I am at once and without
ceremony swept into a hospitality as multilingual as it is inter-
national as it is generous, ancient, permanent: you have only to
enter Santa Maddalena – an illusion which persists with gathering force for the next forty days and nights – to have been there
for ever.

Beatrice is the widow of a writer hailing from central Europe:
Gregor von Rezzori known as Grisha. My fellow writer in
residence is John Burnham Schwartz, now on his third novel.
Our well-being is assured by Intissar the Lebanese cook whose
young family are kept strictly quiet. The talk at lunch as the local
red enlivens the tongue is of a Russian poet here last month, of
Bruce Chatwin and Edmund White, one or both of whom once
slept in my given bed, of Chaucer and Froissart, of modern
fiction and what to read, of Boccaccio and where to find him.

That afternoon I wander down to the signal tower. It is
fourteenth-century, four storeys tall, high ceilings, a flat roof,
steep stairs, thick walls. Each floor can with ease accommodate a
writer, but is now empty and cool. Beds where masterpieces lay
in the making are vacant. Kitchens that fed the wolf of an idea

have turned-off fridges. I sit at various desks where an amoeba of
inspiration sought to evolve out of the primeval mud of a few
notes on an envelope. And I wonder, back to the signalling that
carried the world news north or south from the top of this tower,
how to field my own urgent messages from within or without.

The Penguin translation of *The Decameron* was on my bedside
table, as were in generous selection Grisha's books, one written
entirely without commas. On that first night I skimmed the
Boccaccio in a search for its structure. I had remembered it as a
serial tragicomedy, indeed a hard-edged soap, in which the
characters changed from one episode to the next, but the mood
was always light, wicked, witty. Treading on television's heels, I
thought of reading one a night of the hundred stories at precisely
the same hour, treating it as an addiction, unable to bear missing
an instalment on the stroke of, say, six o'clock.

Here, as in Chaucer, the framework was a pilgrimage, but in
this case more to safety than to worship. Florence was in the
grip of the Black Death, no more virulent description of which
exists than in Boccaccio's dramatic introduction to the first day.
His account was so deadly that I could not believe that
Florence was not still blackened by the taint of plague, rather
than by tourists whose infestation of the city I was warned to
dread.

In the face of death the aim of his art was to get all life stuffed
in. At the church of Santa Maria Novella he assembled his cast, a
septet of virgins and their trio of hopeful studs: youth, the future,
the classy sort of person to whom Froissart might have bowed.
Boccaccio, to keep their minds off the worst as they ride out of
the city's risks, set them a topic for each day, on which each in

turn must tell a story; Chaucer's Host was not quite so bossy.
The topics are those most designed to arouse rage or sex or fear,
any strong emotion to distract a young person from the threat of
his groin suppurating or black boils invading her face. On the
first day, to lull them into his hidden intentions, Boccaccio
offered them a free choice of story to tell.

That was just to get their brains in and tongues loose. He then
posed a real challenge to sedate their fear of infection.

On the second day, girls and boys (Boccaccio pulling strings
on the sidelines), look at yourselves as playthings of a fate that, if
benevolent at all, is only so at the last minute – and tell a good
tale about it. Next day, come up with an anthology of people's
ways of turning destiny to their advantage. As the sun rises on the
fourth, be really daring and give us, in a well-turned storyline,
your varying views of love as a destructive force. At the halfway
point of this escape from contagion, in as many examples as you
can muster, treat love as an enemy that can be exploited for
profit, and see what that does for your vaunted innocence.

On the sixth day, all of you, pull out a few stops to prove that
language has the power to alter the course of events. After a good
night's sleep enjoy yourselves to the utmost with a pyrotechnic
display of the tricks played by adulterous wives on their hus-
bands, again showing the gamut of human ingenuity in the
interests of change. Let day eight be given to a study of every
form, shape, stamp, sort, calibre and type of deception in the war
between the sexes.

Next there will be an open topic after a day's rest, time for you
to choose your special subject, darlings, and on the tenth day,
incubation over, nobody breaking out in pustules, youth's
beauty unassailed by the waste of disease, let fly any story

you want to tell about liberality, a virtue sapped by the plague, but like love an irrational subject, a source of narrative likely to be rich in mendacity as well as suspense.

The Black Death was a lucky chance for Boccaccio. Not only did he survive it. It presented him with a masterpiece.

Again this afternoon, drawn to it, I limp down to the signal tower, into an indolent sunlight filtered by trees which turn out to be figs. The fruit is ripe. The leaves hang low to edit the sun.

A stone bench stands under the widely spreading fig, its branches reaching over a drop into an olive grove descending in terraces towards a gorge. It is vertiginous to a fault. A round table also of stone stands at the edge of the escarpment. Bushes of sage and rosemary thrive against the foot of the tower, this early monument to speedy communications, as signals wave or flame back and forth from one eminence to the next the jubilant or tragic length of Italy. The fists clench in pleasure at the sight of it all.

At last I have begun to find Boccaccio's place.

There is a hunt on. The air is packed with shots remote and close, echoes zigzagging. I long to join the hunters, while pretending to disapprove, sensing the excitement that resounds behind the page I am reading. Troops of baying dogs and gangs of men straining and shouting criss-cross the gorges. This reading of Boccaccio seems to be happening in the century in which he wrote. To bring me back to sense, I abruptly wonder why I should not choose to be conveying Boccaccio to myself on a patio at the rear of a semi on the three-lane A3 in Tolworth, Surrey.

That, after all, is the aim: bringing closer to home the beginnings of the whole process, forcing me to make the effort of imagination to produce my own media; democratising art to the ebullient extent of letting everyone shape art for, and keep the results to, himself. A printed page is a signal tower sending out messages that can be taken in exactly the way you want. Any painting is the view from your window.

The noises I am hearing, which also resound through the brilliantly illuminated pages of *The Hunting Book of Gaston Phoebus*, are the cries that have inhabited these woodlands since long before even this tower was erected. The men below me in the valley are descendants of those who have known Giovanni Boccaccio as that stern minor landowner up the hill, who likes peace and quiet. The hunt veers away. In the uproar of that anarchy of the struggle between man and beast, I am listening exactly to the voice of the moment when Boccaccio either applauded the hunters home to a pitcher of wine or saw their homecoming sidelong from a window, against a tapestry of the very landscape I am looking at now, and put them into a story.

I sit on the stone bench close to the round table and despair of ever seeing the obvious. At this level the late sun shines through the backlit grasses, its blaze blackened by a defining line of cypresses. The dying light illumines a dazzle of insect life, a population of millions dancing before my eyes. Under them bumble bees, a threat of thunder in their tone, move in heavy darts between blooms on the thyme. The opaque hands of fig leaves finger the last of the day. It is most peaceful until I again see, too slippery to be caught or shot or cured, the advent of the plague of the media.

★   ★   ★

The square of Santa Maria Novella [says the guidebook] was inaugurated in 1287, with a decree of the Florentine Republic, and donated to the Church for its ornamentation.

Arranged into lawn beds only a few dacedes *(sic)* ago, since Medieval times the Square was a theatre for festivities, jousts and other events . . . The Facade of the church (Fig 1), facing towards the south, rises gracefully and imposingly. The lower part dates to the middle of the XIV century.

Even a fanatic might find this hard reading over a breakfast of dry toast and thin tea on the morning of setting off for his first visit to Florence. On a side table sat today's *New York Herald Tribune* fetched early from Donnini. By resisting the paper I found to my gladness a reference to Boccaccio on page 54 of the guide. He was on a fresco in the very church that breathed life into his book.

From San Ellero I go for the 10.17 a.m. to Florence, parking with the dispatch of a commuter, climbing into a full train, its rolling stock half a century old, redolent of rivieras. The seats are of generous leather. Long mirrors below the luggage racks show you fast receding the views which at the window you have just seen approaching, a dizzying conversion of present to past.

An olive-skinned girl is reading a book of strip cartoons. One man with a square face and oily looks I appoint a temporary stand-in for Boccaccio. For the half-hour of the journey the European travel of my twenties is evoked by the quadrilingual order not to lean out of the window. We draw into the terminus parallel to a Eurostar, at 10.55 departing for Napoli; any rival chasing Boccaccio's youth has plenty of time to catch it.

From the terminus at Santa Maria Novella to the eponymous church is a short limp, past the stalls selling tourist tat, dull *panini* and cheap wine: no temptation. Smoke curls from a brazier of chestnuts: almost irresistible. A squatting beggar projects a plump hand across the pavement as if to trip you up, at least morally. I am not to be deflected, because I know where Boccaccio is.

I am to meet him at last face to face, the guidebook has promised. He is pictured on a fresco in the Cappelone degli Spagnoli. The way lies through the peace and immensity of the Chiostro Verde, the completion of which immaculately proportioned cloister the plague interrupted in the 1340s. You are slowed down by a true beauty of an open space. Each regular cypress exclaims against the hot sun, hiding frescoes that have flaked into the seeming modernity of abstracts. You sense your sense of time ebbing.

I quietly enter the Spanish Chapel, only to rock back on my ankle.

From top to toe, on all sides, east, west, south, north, this chapter house is all colour, design, image, vigour. Nothing is unpainted. At a stroke I am visually hurled into Boccaccio's universe. Whichever way I turn the events of the gospels are painted in all their extremes of drama, some tucked into corners of the square apse round the altar, lots taking place up in the vault. On the left Christ's entry into Jerusalem is being ignored by a couple of lads who, in an artist's trick, are peering down at the next setpiece below, which is Christ carrying the Cross: a film cut, leading the eye further into the story, which soon develops into a scrimmage of hellish monsters as Christ passes through limbo. Above my head Christ ascends vertiginously into

a heaven foreshortened by its very proximity. Heaven is un-
nervingly close.

Every echo of association in a long life of attempts to deal with
this florid faith – kneeling to pray at a childhood bed in
Hampshire, drafting my own elegies in many a country churchyard, onward into maturity's stances of disbelief that never left
me or anyone else happy – is swept to the side by the totality of
this vision. A fast-moving cartoon is brainstorming me at a
glance, forcing me to think again, shifting me out of the usual
doubts by the very intensity of the execution, every detail
telling. The force of it, the success, springs from the overall
coverage, at the speed required by fresco, of the given space. It is
urgent, all this, not old, it's now, yes, it's hold the front page, it's
great television, eminently watchable, the goods. I crick my
neck, I reel backwards from the Crucifixion, I stare at the
Passion; I fidget, change posture, and still can't get enough of
it, abruptly recognising what buildings and which backgrounds I
am seeing. I am in them both. The Holy Land is Tuscany in an
evergreen autumn. The Church is this very one I stand in. It all
happened here; it is all happening here; our religion happens
where we have our being or makes no sense, and I have an
instant charge of the magnificent gobbledegook I have fondly
grown up with, its unbelievable assumptions for ever a part of
my love for life. My spirit is soaked in this propaganda which has
lasted 2,000 years and has never hesitated to use the wiles of the
media to perpetuate its message.

Calm down. No one is here to be converted. Yet, drawn by
those childish old habits to any touch of the numinous, I have
missed the wall that matters, the south wall, the secular element
that brings me up to date. Here I am at home, bang on time and

target, the fourteenth century painted live, as it is being lived. Andrea di Bonaiuto, says the guidebook, is one of the seven invited to construct the dome of the Duomo. In this fresco, a panorama of contemporary Florence, all his own work, he sketches his idea for that dome, a flourish for the future, to top a cathedral otherwise completed. (The dome had to wait for Brunelleschi a century later.) In front of this ideal church, pictured here as if captured on still film, in various attitudes of state and dignity, are the men and women of Andrea's time snapped from the life.

Well below the heavenly host he puts popes and kings into the composition in due order, but also, amid a scurry of dogs, the poets, the poets, and the mistresses who breathed verse into their mouths. Dante stands in profile. Petrarch is full face. Slightly below them – I can't quite bear this encounter, want to look away, not ready for it – is the squarish pink-cheeked face of Giovanni Boccaccio, narrowed and tawny of eye, plump but high cheekboned, solemn, giving little away, as if self-conscious under the spotlight but resolved not to show it. Underneath this trio of giants are grouped their women. Beatrice looks fine, Laura not bad. By far the most seductive of the three, Fiammetta in profile is a dizzy blonde. I know her and never trusted her an inch which was why I was in love. She is so placed by the artist that if Giovanni let his held book slip sideways, in an act of vengeance for all the inspiration she forced on him, his life's work would bounce off her head and floor her.

I am haunted by that look in Boccaccio's eye. He is staring directly at me without favour, even with a measure of mistrust. Was this the period when he was starting to sink into the spells of clinical depression that great artists appear to need? He seems trapped, taut with failure, unwilling to come to terms with the scenes he observes out here in the world. It is hard to get closer to him; his position is too high in the vault; he is hemmed in by his peers or, as he thinks, his superiors, not to say his proximity to the one and only romance that mattered to him, the failure of which he seems to court with acid self-denial. I am consumed with a mad need to tempt him down from the wall, from that fast five-minute fresco when Andrea caught him in the life at a moment of gloom he prefers to forget, the only way for me being to photograph him in huge close-up with a long-focus lens and so enlarge him that I can paste every brush-stroke of his features on the wall of my room or, better, a blank wall of my mind where at once they spring alive in a way that can be studied, analysed, pinned down; even liked.

Out in the cloister I lock this image in memory and decide to stand it a drink. From the café, relieved by a *negroni*, I look across the vast cobbled square, itself as much time as space, and face the fact that I must tap my stick across its uneven surface and enter the tiny door in the huge portal that hides the interior of Santa Maria Novella, the church where Boccaccio launches *The Decameron* at the height of the plague.

The black and white façade still looks exactly as he saw it, give or take a detail, massively constructed in blocks of mint humbug. The back of my mind searches for a reason for not approaching it quite yet: another *negroni* perhaps; but I have already paid. The metal tip of the stick strikes sparks off the cobbles. I step inside with the swagger if not the authority of Boccaccio.

The nave is overwhelmingly tall and cavernous and empty except for a few rows of seats towards the altar. They are

occupied by youth. The boys and girls have on their faces an awe
that is indistinguishable from a blank. They are worshipping
nobody. The stones of the church are staring into their eyes,
which they now cover with cameras to flash the building out of
sight and mind. They are resting from the heat for free.

But out of their groupings the cast I need begins to assemble.
A girl with hair a rich auburn has a hand slung round the
shoulder of an olive-skinned creature whose looks are ruined
only by a backpack looming above her head, straps cutting into
her shoulders, and drab flabby gear on her limbs below: a
shapeless beauty looking desperate. They are whispering about
getting out; the heat is a plague; they need to escape, fresh air,
freedom. Another girl, blonde and loopy, joins them, touching
hands, kissing a fingertip. They gather in my mind, these women
with a timeless if not endless future ahead of them, a future any
moment to be cut off by risk; repetitively they keep whispering
that they long in any order for freedom, fresh air, escape.

They can go it alone. But company would help, a boy or two,
as long as they are not outnumbered. They look around. The
auburn girl, reminding me of someone known in the dark ages
of youth, beckons her into the conspiracy, and I see their instant
accord, a murmur that is beyond hearing; the heart melts, at a
glimpse of their longing to get away from the plague, their belief
that they can make it, their determination, as they touch and kiss,
to bring about every possible relief from all they fear: all it might
be, for all I know, is just what life might do to them.

Boccaccio comes in at the west end, a tiny figure in the
distance. Of course he has brought the girls here. An artist has
assembled them for a formal purpose. He wants to tell stories or
rather to assemble in a potent anthology, more seminally than

ever before, the stories that others have told. He has an urge at once to be encyclopaedist of the world's basic tales, every tragedy, all comedy, and to make them his own, as well as to bring them home locally, by setting them afresh in the known world, the world he knows: this city of Florence radiating outwards to other Italian cities, Certaldo where he thinks he was born, the Naples he believes he loves, and to parts of Greece, north and west into France, as far afield as Africa, to the very point where civilisation falls off the edge of the earth.

He draws nearer in the gloom, walking quickly out of depression into decision. Behind him a team of wardrobe people from a film studio stand ready. Out of the vestry his staff of dressers are running long trolleys hung with even longer clothes which brush dust in clouds off the tiles. A batch of oriental tourists shuffle off, noticing nothing, sure they have caught in their cameras all they need to show at home to prove the fact of this huge fantasy of a building. The ones left, the auburn girl and her small group, a few boys, are drawn to the arrival of Boccaccio, without thinking it odd, despite his diminutive size and the drapes he chooses to wear. A dozen or so hang around loosely on the chairs waiting to be told where to go and what to do, and without a word, using a minimum of gesture, he picks his cast as might a director who knows his mind.

The seven young ladies and three lads stand and lazily draw off the flab of their clothes. The billowing jeans that reek of travel drop to the floor. Bodies fold in half to slip exiguous underwear over their feet. The boys toss aside boxers and await instructions, shapely and shivering in holed socks, ready for adventure. But the author's women come first. Discreetly, behind screens of dresses embellished with threads of gold and silver that glisten as sharply as Boccaccio's all-seeing eye, the girls strip their bodies naked – for a new start, another chance, that ached-for escape, the finding of their true selves in the challenge of an opportunity unlikely to be repeated.

The wardrobe people gather round them, slipping over their heads the rich stuffs that fall in folds at their feet, pampering their breasts with silk, smoothing their hips. Suddenly they are clothed as never before. They are alive in a heightened key, and you can see it in their innocence, the outer beauty expressing more than a hint of the inner. You can see it in their eyes.

Boccaccio retires a pace or two to reflect. He has set the scene for capturing the world in a series of stories. The spare garments are rolled away by the wardrobe mistress into the oblivion of the vestry. The grubby attire of universal tourism is scooped up by extras playing dustmen and taken off to the dump. The church is silent and empty and shut for lunch. Outside in the hot intestines of the city the likes of me, trippers trapped in time, sit at open-air tables washing down pasta with crude wine, gazing open-mouthed at newspapers, suckers for tonight's television. Something must be done about the horror that is gripping us all.

As an author Boccaccio is at liberty to put thoughts into these nice young people's minds, words into their mouths, make them realise that their only hope of survival is to get out of town fast. Quickly they must lay hands on some of the few remaining horses. They must hire grooms and find servants. They have to be looked after, these messengers to the future. They need to be guided to a safe place to stay, a place in accord with their elegance, their good looks. After all, they are to be entrusted with the responsibility of telling one another the range of the world's greatest stories, in competition, the stories that touch the funny bone as tenderly as they strike into the heart of things, the anecdotes that elbow religion, the tales that mock the peaks of pretension and chasms of folly which for the next half-millennium, to say the least, is to render human affairs sad, if comical, also contemptible. So reflects Boccaccio. And so say I.

Yes, we are together. Giovanni knows we are on safe ground. The young persons he has reclothed for his purposes in Santa Maria Novella are of mixed or different races. One of the girls is French by birth but half-Italian, more than one comes from further north, a county lass from Hampshire who in former times qualified as a deb but is now tramping her way into maturity, a blonde plainly from Sweden, a woman from Argentina whose English is a polyglot mixture of South-American Spanish and Italian, others living all over the place but of Latin extraction or Greek, a boy just down from Oxford after reading modern languages and pretending his Italian is not up to much: all communicate. They share the same language. They nod, blow a kiss, gesticulate, try a word, fail, get it wrong, try again, bother, want to make it, succeed; it is like making love to understand totally what a person is saying and what you say back. For the first time, and for the glorious explosion of finding your voice, they are into the vernacular. They all are into each other, so who cares where they come from – they wear the same attitudes, they bear the same packs on their backs. And now he, Giovanni Boccaccio, the author, is rescuing them from a death worse than fate's normal array: infection from a flea jumping off the back of a rat leaping off a ship hailing from parts of the world from which any one of these youngsters might have derived her or his origin.

For fear of being himself infected by some unknown factor he cannot control, Giovanni steps out of Santa Maria Novella. He keeps his cast on hold within. He needs somewhere else to consider their future. He has them in his mind; they will wait for him. Off he strides in search of provender to think it all out. A great idea has struck him. Gone are the poems of yesteryear, the old ideas, the copycat versions of writers so ancient as to be best forgotten. This is a modern idea; he has his finger on the pulse of the here and now.

The Florentine streets are crowded with people pouring out of offices in search of lunch. He joins them, mixes with them, is proud to be in their midst. Behind the plate-glass windows along the Via Tornabuoni stand the models in their up-to-the-minute fashions as Boccaccio hurries past, awaiting his beck and call, to spring into motion at a moment's notice. Before the Ponte Vecchio he turns into streets as narrow as canyons, where the whizz of scooters reasserts the present, on his way to a familiar restaurant. The alleys between are dashing with youth in a hurry, quick embraces, the click of chic footwear on cobbles.

At one of I Latini's tables for eight or ten I take a place in the middle, flanked by two oriental girls in mirror image at one end. Opposite sits the figure fresh in my mind of Boccaccio, his features still glum, his mien depressed. In front of us stands one of the table's two-litre flasks of Val d'Este, the house wine, to be drunk at will in any quantity for next to nothing. In good companionship I order and eat prosciutto and salami, then a ravioli stuffed with spinach and ricotta, while coming to terms with how to escape this stricken city. Out of the corner of my eye I note a very thin man at the table wolfing an overdone lamb chop six inches thick, and at once I see that everything in sight is seen and felt by Boccaccio: wheat, wood, cheese, vegetables, cloth, spices, wine, language of his senses, his basics of the commonplace. We are on terms.

Boccaccio has seen the plague on these hot streets of his. But how to instil it as a source of fear in these young people, a fear strong enough to get them off their butts, brush up their manners, acquaint them with elegance to go with their ideals, civilise them to the point at which he can put stories into their mouths and stand back? What is a contemporary threat strong enough in them to drive them out of town in fear of their lives?

He had come into Santa Maria Novella wondering himself how to escape. He knew other cities, of course – he had spent years in Naples, Certaldo he knew well – but they were likely to be no less infected than Florence, perhaps worse. It was reported on all sides that you were safer from contamination if you lived in the country. For the sake of your skin you had to risk spreading a disease of which traces might already lurk in your blood. A church had a specious air of sanctuary from evil; you entered one neither to pray nor worship but to take refuge in the silence that bandaged the running sore of being alive. He had not expected therein to come across the kernel of his idea for *The Decameron*; but, as soon as he saw the kids, he knew.

He, Giovanni Boccaccio, will harness their fears to his own. He will teach them to see for real the horror in their hearts and, as an artist must, relieve them, succour and sweeten them, until instead of brooding inwardly on their neuroses they are out- wardly telling one another his stories, trotting out into the Tuscan landscape on horses as well trained and docile as this cross-section of sexy youth is now becoming, thanks only to him. In that moment the cloud of his bitter dread, the bad weather that has haunted his life, lifts. He sees that by chance he has stumbled upon the threshold of what is best in him.

The next point to settle is where to take his captives. There is the farm at Settignano where he makes his wine, but the premises are too cramped, not grand enough for the plans he has in mind for the triumph of their arrival. Above it, looking down on the hazy narrows of the Arno valley widening towards Florence, stands the more commanding outlines of the villa I Tatti, hidden within a coppice of cypresses, occupied from 1900 until his death fifty-nine years later by the art critic Bernard Berenson; anachronism, thought Boccaccio, is never an issue if the story is good enough to sustain it. The annexe to the 1907 library, all panelled in sepia in the faded photograph, contains many an upright sarcophagus known as a bookcase which immures Boccaccio and his work, his boring endless verses, any number of even more tedious critics, and a concordance.

He can keep this quiet. There will be no need for any of the beauties to use the library, still less their beaux. Nobody reads nowadays. The view from the terrace is at the very least inspiring. They can just about see in the distance the seething inferno of death that is the city they have just left. By craning their necks they will make out the television aerials fretting the dome of the Duomo in a foreshortening of those hundreds of housetop hieroglyphs. Anyway, I Tatti is worth a try, even if he has to move them on to better quarters later.

I Latini charges us eight quid. Men pay from whacks of notes dragged from fat pockets on fatter bottoms. You get a slap on the shoulder from a passing waiter. Democracy is here to stay as long as the vernacular keeps it going; this is like eating at home if noisier; noise has its own privacy. I look out on Florentine colours, faded sunlight washed on walls, shutters echoing tree green. Plants waterfall off balconies in alleys as narrow as side aisles. On the back of the guide to Santa Maria Novella is a medieval version of this exact scene, a printout of a city that has yet to vanish behind transport: vespas buzzing, bikes, hum of motors, stink of fuel, scents of freedom. In an old building a girl is watering window boxes that snow white petals on to the cobbles.

Giovanni has left me flat and gone back to Santa Maria Novella to get the youngsters geared up and tell them in no uncertain terms that they can only save their bacon by thinking up a competitive story or two, behaving like ladies and gentlemen for once, and getting the hell out of Firenze.

Day after day I grow used to the route by car to the libraries in and around Florence which contain all history and bunk. From San Ellero the road winds at perilous speed into a channel between shaggy hills, asking for accidents, then sharpens into a funnel as the hills narrow, inviting panic, and after Pontassieve the road closely follows the course of the Arno, railway running alongside, river churning below, trains roaring overhead on the grey stilts of viaducts. Road, water, rail: communications on the ground summarised in triplicate. A glum morning of the thick mists that enclose Santa Maddalena clears into a miracle of light as I drive down to I Tatti at Settignano. It is the Italian round-the-clock rush hour, all fourteen hours of it.

The road to the Middle Ages is narrow, with alluring lanes leading off it to half-seen farms. A plaque embedded in a wall pulls me up sharp. It names the notables, from Michelangelo and Leigh Hunt to Mark Twain, John Addington Symonds and d'Annunzio, who have turned Settignano into a ghetto of fame. Over time they have lolled in these hills, fighting off manic depression or spouses or local hate or writer's block while going through the motions of paradise. In climbing these foothills of Elysium, care is needed to avoid the vans hurtling back to earth on hairpin bends. 'I Tatti', suddenly says a sign.

Security responds to the touch of a button and a pair of modern gates swing open. A few steps and here, as in a hospital, is reception; here a passage to the wards where the books lie on trolleys and stack up and lie open and half-dead on tables; here a number of scholars engage in the diagnosis of minutiae.

It is all as silent as if the worst were feared. Not unpleasurably, for I am still alive, my heart sinks. These experts have an air of contained emergency as they go about curing an obsession with books. Shoulders bent by Cambridge, eyes glazed by Yale, brains as computerised as the catalogue, they note their references and set off at an urgent slant for the shelves. Ignoring the parallelograms of sun filtered from the skylights, they move towards desks lit by table lamps in bays soundproofed by books, more books to the floor, books darkening to the roof, and the ruminative silence is the sound of the twenty-first century chewing on its roots, in the highly academic hope of new growth arising from a digestion of the past.

To my eye every book visible, in however rich a prose or binding, looks too late to be of any use. I am out of the habit of libraries. I never twigged that my effort to reconcile the weight of the past with the flightiness of the present would land me back in class. Horrors, I am now about to back into the piles of schoolbooks ink-stained and dog-eared. With leaden tread I am trudging into the Radcliffe Camera where broody girls sit on

books that will never hatch. I mount the heavy steps to the
Christ Church library which exhales asphyxiating dust and
exhumes unreadable masterpieces and expects original thought.
I panic slightly. Paper and print are about death, including your
own, each book enshrining a last will and testament with never a
last-minute codicil in your favour.

I take hold. The finest part of this library consists of the two
vaulted chambers built on Berenson's orders in 1907 to house his
collection which eventually ran to 30,000 volumes. Now there are
120,000. With courtesy I am told by a passing egghead that I shall
need to master the catalogue on screen. It will give me instant
access to the Library of Congress. I press a button, with a touch of
guilt as if turning on television by day, to be sharply told that I
cannot send personal messages; the computer then jams, incri-
minating me. I nip off with a resolve to treat this well-ordered den
of research as one of the tumble of bookshops in my boyhood,
half-hidden in somewhere like Canterbury, where I missed the
obvious but stumbled on secrets. I roam the stacks on foot.

On my desk I pile the books up. A paragraph at random tells
me that after Dante (died 1321) nothing seems beyond human
reach, a view also taken by Boccaccio (born 1313). I do some
revision; facts get forgotten. By his merchant father the young
Giovanni was despatched to a bank in Naples, where he saw, fell
for, watched, courted, stalked his girlish ideal Fiammetta. Fiammetta! She is the heartache throbbing in all his poetical works
that nobody reads, the equivalent of Dante's Beatrice or Petrarch's Laura. This trio of lovelorn authors projected on to these
ladies, in pair upon pair of couplets, the blame for withholding
their favours, poor sweethearts, not their fault, they were just too
classy to be available.

A further delve into the pile amply confirms that Boccaccio's mother is French – was he not born in Paris? In old age she no doubt ignored Froissart in the street, or cut Chaucer when he visited Picardy on a peace mission, or grimaced at Machaut's music when he was a canon at Reims; any guess may be as good as mine, but I am not good at concentrating in libraries. The limbs seize up.

Boccaccio's early career is a bit like Chaucer's a few years later. He is a municipal councillor. Later he represents his city in Brandenburg in 1351 and is Florence's ambassador to the Pope at Avignon (1354 and 1365), his very posts confirming him as courtier, scholar, man of the world. Seemingly his first novel, *Filocolo*, had its 600 pages read all over Europe, but by what means of distribution and by how many people? My ankle is aching from all that stretching to the shelves. He penned nine more works of fiction. His life of Dante had wide (but among whom?) circulation. I begin to seek escapes.

One's own faults gape when one tries to get to grips with a one-man culture like Boccaccio putting his head down to achieve total understanding not only of his own epoch but of eras past. He digs out of hiding authentic texts by such Romans as Martial and Tacitus. He translates Livy into Italian in the time it takes me to watch the nightly news on television for a couple of months. While I accumulate rewards at the supermarket in hour upon hour of shopping, Boccaccio puts together a topography of the ancient world from alpha to omega. I spend afternoons bogged down in old movies on the box or catching up obituaries in the broadsheets, while his *Genealogies of the Pagan Gods* takes the deities of the classical world back to their origins, thus offering to the up-and-coming Renaissance a basic text to inspire its outburst of art in word and paint and stone: his book's authority is to last half a millennium. Does this pain of a polymath never have doubts? Has he never suffered from failures of energy or nerve? A thunderhead of boredom settles over my brain.

Then I open a story by Boccaccio (Day VIII, Story 3) at random. Instead of close print driving me to learning, the page urges me into the erotic. At once he joins Chaucer among the first men to whip the curtains back on romantic love to revel in the randy. A foretaste of the modern lurks in every paragraph waiting to spring into the open. Impersonal artifice and allegory are slipping out of writing; individuals are being asked to face up to themselves. The theory now is: I visualise, therefore I identify. Boccaccio has seen the light: let us tell stories for they consist of an equal degree of pleasure and utility. 'Al novellare torneremo,' he says, 'nel qual mi par grandissima parte di piacere e d'utilità similmente consistere.'

This story – an abbot drugs a rich businessman into a coffin while consorting with his wife and persuades him that he has awoken in purgatory – is a relief but, hemmed in by the stuffy virtue of Berenson's books, I seem to be reading it in the wrong place. I am breathless with a longing to rescue it. Its libido will stifle here in this library. I must carry all this lust into the open air where its heart and loins can start pumping again.

The doors to Berenson's quarters were locked except to librarians; you needed a combination or a swipecard to reach the heights of early Renaissance art that not only bedecked his walls but projected out of their gorgeous colour the last of the mindset of Boccaccio's world.

My moment was to come. One day my hostess at Santa Maddalena fiercely recommended me to ring up the director of I Tatti, soon to return from fundraising in America. I felt slightly pestered: my research was my own; but this man would be a revelation, she said, with a hint that I might need any I could get. An old friend's letter then turned up from New England to say that on no account must I miss him. When I suspected he was back, a natural disposition to leave people alone (unless they were long-dead fathers of the media) paralysed me. On my visits to the library I knew he must be somewhere at I Tatti: an added buzz, despite the silence, staff on their toes, an awe. Through keyholes escaped scents of cooking that forced me out of research to seek lunch downhill in the village trattoria.

Meanwhile, from vulgar curiosity, it was the spirit, or rather spectre, of Bernard Berenson (1865–1959) which deflected my mind from its work in his library. A little man with a pointed beard, not unlike Lenin, he too had an ideal, in his case to create in his own home, for students in their twenties, 'a lay monastery for leisurely culture'. He wanted the culture of the future to mature its talents under his roof, its gifts as talkers and writers. Otherwise 'a dreary abstraction will reign', he said, 'and who will preside, what kind of biped will replace me and mine?'

He shrank from the media. More than half a century ago Berenson knew the fight was on. Among the bipeds he entertained as friends and guests were numbered Bertrand Russell, Lytton Strachey, Logan Pearsall Smith, André Gide, Paul Valéry, George Santayana, Gabriele d'Annunzio, Isaiah Berlin, Benedetto Croce ('more the Duce in matters of the mind than Mussolini ever was in politics'), Edith Wharton, Yehudi Menuhin. They lunched, they talked, they made music, in these cavernous halls of the highest standards of art: the genuine, the first-hand, the first-rate in its class, were the only levels that mattered, as yet another fine hint of a meal escaped the keyhole and turned me unsteady with appetite.

I take heart and ring the director. At once he invites me to lunch. I feel elected to an exclusive club, conducting its culture on the fine-drawn line where visual and verbal meet in friendly clash, less as opponents than as competitors. Although I Tatti is a world library built and constantly growing on Berenson's foundations, the crucial language of the house is painting, the pictures Berenson spent his life collecting; the books are just annotation or footnotes. Amid all the talk you are left in no doubt that brush strokes speak louder than words – perspectives extend to greater depth than any amount of prose, which in any case diminishes in effect the more you use of it: a picture hits once.

The fellows at I Tatti, fifteen a year, gather for a quick drink (martini, *punt-è-mes*, tomato juice) before lunch at a refectory table, no time wasted, the director at the head, a joint of pork and apple sauce, roast potatoes, very good, a green salad and fruit, very crisp, wine from vineyards down below the villa, very *buvable*, says mine host; Boccaccio knew and made and drank it. The head reels over the intimacy of the taste, as if smelling the warmth of the past's breath.

The director is as I imagined him, even in physical structure, and I at once fall in with his cast of mind; our New England friend, a woman differently fond of us both, seems present in our talk. His speech has enthusiasm, his manner impatience. He will suffer no fool gladly, if at all. I think of being on these terms with Boccaccio – whose life and work this ex-professor once taught at

Harvard – or any other of my more or less irrecoverable men 600 years old, who yet suddenly keep turning up, at once recognisable, friends of friends of mine, companions as good as this.

I watch the director sluice a mouthful of wine between his keen judicious sentences. He has already told me that after half a millennium (just as the view from the window of Boccaccio's villa is largely unaltered) that draught of wine inflicts the same sensations on his palate as it did on Boccaccio's; the same earth is buried in it, the same sun rounds off the grapes that went into its making, the same rough cellarage keeps it firm over a winter. I too drink. The wine has strength and mettle. Closing my eyes briefly to appreciate its flavour seems to mean that I can shut my eyes to time too; it is all one in the depths of the here and now: being alive *in toto* is all.

Back at Santa Maddalena I again try to start reading a story by Boccaccio. I am not into the idiom. I am missing the mood. Where am I? In an isolation full of noises, this morning has been thrown into neurosis by an eager maid who dashes about the upstairs with a rush of footfalls that clack on tile. She fades into the past, then clatters back into the present. Her heels tap out a headache as Boccaccio slips out of my grip by a back door. It is all overhead, where the brain is supposed to be. This maid, under Froissart's brooding glance, will soon be promoted manageress of that hotel in Valenciennes.

Meanwhile I cast her as a victim in the same episode of a soap that stars the secretive to-and-fro of the Lebanese servants. She moves silkenly, he pads like a hunter. Curtains float on the air as the sole sign of their recent passage. Their children are kept mum in a barn that might be a hundred years away from the

house but is ten yards. Roaming dogs now and then roar to the
defence of our solitude against unknown odds or intruders. It is
the setting for a Boccaccio story; here at Santa Maddalena we
are assembling a good set of ingredients – anger, mystery, sexual
secrets, a touch of barbaric threat, civilisation's ironies. What
more do you want?

Giovanni is aware of the lives teeming around him as a
novelist must be, of life's nuisance value, its arrant lack of point,
its need to be picked up and given a good shaking for being so
mischievous and dumb, as well as the inner torture of having to
get life into order, order of the pure technical kind which a
joiner feels when faced with wood and tools, making an object
small and neat out of a wilderness large and formless – and once
in a lifetime, if as often, coming up with an artefact to match or
rival or beat life in all its aspects of pain, indifference, treachery,
futility, charm, bossiness, wonder.

In the quest I move further afield. Daily I continue my search for
a place to read a Boccaccio story so that it will echo back from
the past with a resonance that enlivens the present. I take the
train south down the Arno valley to Arezzo, if only because just
one of the stories is set in that city, despite its distinctive place in
Boccaccio's mind as the town and birthplace of his revered
Petrarch. Well contained on a slope, the city has a main artery
rising to a piazza, into which flow medieval capillaries of paved
alley or narrow street. In these environs a film famed in the
media, *La Vita è Bella*, was recently shot; it is easier to find
plaques that record the location of a particular scene than to feel
your way unguided to Petrarch's home.

In a medieval passage a restaurant provides a setting for this story (Day VII, Story 4) set in Arezzo: an odd little tale. In this very street, you imagine, a husband who drinks suspects his wife of infidelity. So ennobled by rage is she that she warmly encourages him to get more and more sloshed, so that she can indeed launch the affair of which she has been falsely accused. One night he traps her by staying sober and shutting her out of the house. She takes her revenge by pretending to throw herself in despair down the well in the courtyard, whereupon he rushes forth, she dashes inside and locks him out. All ends with the making of an amicable arrangement between them.

On the banquette my first thought is that I am watching television. Here is a straight two-hander, throbbing with undertones of sex, which twists and turns its way to a rounded conclusion. But, visually though I have seen every frame of the story, the action is taking place in my brain with only a few deft hints from the author. I am inventing it as I go along, his words my key to the images I make.

In a story powered by alcohol I have read those words surrounded by drink, for the walls are a tight-packed library of bottles, standing upright like books on shelves to the ceiling, their names as appetising as titles on a spine. Also holding an assortment of bottles is a long table which produces a dramatic incident worthy of Boccaccio himself. When I am well into a carpaccio of cheese topped with tomato, lots of wine bottles on that table, halves and wholes, start skittling over, crashing about, dropping on to chairs, clanging together, falling to the floor, as if they were drunk.

Whodunnit? The waiter, a bespectacled figure as academic in looks as the storyteller. All is quickly righted, but I keep an eye

on this waiter as a character not only prone to accident but
created by a master of caricature.

Stories and actuality continue to wrestle and nearly coincide.
In the train to Florence, intending to read another Boccaccio
story, I fail. The retina is resistant to print. The sinuous reality
beyond the window is more complicated than a story. Here and
now the Arno valley is as narrow and thunderous as a horror
movie. The structure of the half-hour ride into the city is classic:
a beginning at San Ellero where in a downpour I await the train,
a middle after Pontassieve where hills close in like the weather,
trees lash, until soon a climax must be reached and, goodness, it
opens out ahead; I already know the end but it is always a source
of astonishment – yes, Florence! If the journey is a story I follow
with my eye, I get a running commentary from other occupants
of the compartment in Italian, a code to some greater mystery
only in theory within my grasp: a message. I miss reading a story,
but for thirty minutes the landscape has made up a real one,
which at once, in the excitement of the arrival platform at Santa
Maria Novella, feels like fiction lodged in my mind by a master.

I break my hurry from the station for an espresso at the empty
Giacosa; one young woman at a remove, munching a croissant
in a napkin, is too sensibly sad for a story by Boccaccio. Outside
the drabness of big business bites into the bones, the buildings
look monumentally nordic, the glassy stores along the Villa
Tornabuoni are still shut, though I mistake their subtly lit models
for shop assistants. The whole length of the street is populated by
ghosts of fashion, the beauties in *The Decameron* redressed to the
nines. The Arno is crossed by a bridge bombed when I was
fourteen.

At the Harold Acton library the vertical sliding ladder, to find

the best of Boccaccio on the very top shelf, is a labour. You look
down at your peril. Why is he so far away? It feels like climbing a
sheer cliff with only one leg in the search for an enlightenment
never to be won. Chairs scrape on the floor with the shriek of
fingernails on glass, umbrellas clash at the street door, Vespas
scoot past with a swoosh. Florence can have been no less rackety
with intimations of panic when Boccaccio was sketching his ten
days of escape from the plague. I rest my ankle and thought on a
dozy reminder of what the old boy set out to do. The whole of
Boccaccio's plan of escape from the plague, day after day, is the
first and classiest version of the last and longest run of a dozen
channels of soaps that for decades have grabbed millions all over
the world, and by taking over our brains half kill us. The seizure
of this thought would get anyone to his feet with a wild squeak
of the chair.

The library is stuffy, rain floods the glass, the Arno races, I long
for air; I also long for a story with as distinct a need as for lunch.
Out I tumble into the wind, Boccaccio in the shoulder bag, to be
blown down alleys deeper into inner San Felicità – Boccaccio's
own neighbourhood – eyes weeping against the weather,
blurring outlines of the medieval, drizzle dashing across the
specs. Outside the Quattro Leoni, as I hasten out of the rain into
the restaurant, the piazza is waiting to be peopled, nobody about,
scene for a story. With a swallow of *bianco* Boccaccio's story is
ready to be read.

I am a Florentine merchant in Paris who has only to hear of a
matchless woman in Bologna to fall at once in love with her. A
quick glance at the women at other tables proves them largely
American. So I drop my life of rich privilege and worm my way
into her husband's service in a humble capacity, just as a waiter

sets before me a veal chop. In due course I take advantage of my
employer's absence out hunting and reveal my love – whereupon I am seemingly exposed by my paragon. But this is only to
find that she has devised a more cunning stratagem for adultery
that I can hit on, and it is so witty and such fun, and ends so well,
that in and out of my lunch I keep smiling at the large American
women at neighbouring tables; while they take me for tipsy or
cracked I think how equally close to life here and now are the
words I am reading to the sights I am seeing: arches in brick
vaulting overhead, walls patched and plastered, soft-beat jazz so
low-key I can mistake it for a lute being plucked fairly far off in
some palazzo.

On the return to the Harold Acton a grand moment occurs by
chance. In an alley hardly wide enough for the three-wheel
motorised cart that forces me, umbrella high in the air, to back
on to the six-inch pavement, I glance at an arch with half a roll-
up grille raised and glimpse within the secret glints of a treasure
chest: mirrors from down the centuries, bric-a-brac reflected in
the glitter of those mirrors, which also image the gleam of glass
cabinets with precious trifles in them. I have no instant idea of
anything's value except as a spectacle, but much better than any
riches, sitting in his den, presides their guardian, the spider both
comic and sly at the focus of the web.

He is an ample man who for a second with a smile lifts his eyes
from his reading and meets mine, again as in a mirror. In that
second, for no reason but a good one, I identify him with
Boccaccio; his looks swim into me, a contact the more living for
being so brief. I pass on; I have to, there is no excuse to stay, let
alone to watch, only then judging that for a metphorical instant I
have gazed deep into the fourteenth century and caught it being

as profound an illusion as the present. I let down my umbrella as
the ancient rains bustle me into the library for further revelations.

The next story Boccaccio tells is on the train back to Santa
Maddalena in the dusk. Two youngish women are in urgent
chatter as I find the page. The Arezzo express curls at minimum
speed round the lamped outskirts of Florence. The lights are dim
enough to strain the eyes.

One of the story's women, leaning into the leather of this
rolling stock surviving from old Europe's crack trains, is a nice
Arab girl from Tunisia who hears about God and wants to know
more. The views over the Arno fade as she labours off into the
desert to discover a Christian hermit who will come up with the
truth, preferably by our first stop at Campo di Marte.

The action pauses while people alight into a dismal suburb and
other extras take their place on board. Keeping to her corner,
still puzzled by God, the nice Arab girl is handed on by her first
adviser, who is consumed by fears of lust, to a guru equally
protective of his moral code, until at last, as we draw into
Rovezzano where nobody gets off, she meets a fine young
hermit, as subtle as he is virile, who convinces her, not to
mention me, that the only way to find release for the evil in him
is to thrust the devil into the very hell that occupies the same hot
area of her hitherto unvisited body. To understand and appease
God, he argues, the errant prick must be consigned to the
equally sinful cunt.

Nobody pulls the communication cord. I look out at the blur
of a passing cypress. Not a soul in the compartment looks at all
embarrassed, least of all the nice Arab girl who is curled into her
corner half asleep, tired by the exertions of chatter. I half see a

gorge swallowed up by the darkening night. I sigh with pleasure as we zoom into San Ellero and home. Giovanni has done it again: enriched the present by a wink from the past.

I am off on pilgrimage to Boccaccio's home during his last years, his deathbed. The drive across Tuscany is slow, but then, racing up from the Middle Ages, like writing that makes sense, as cubist as a painting of it, in a notation as four-square as plainsong, there on its height is inscribed against the sky the marvel of the outline of Certaldo.

Boccaccio's city or citadel is not easy to approach. The modern town swirls round the foot of the hill as if besieging the old. The narrow lane angled upwards to Boccaccio's retirement is signposted so late as to invite a pile-up. Beyond a suburb that peters out, the circuitous route – or road rather, no, lane, if more of a track – to the Middle Ages rises, unkempt olive trees wriggling down into valleys that lift into ranks of trim vines, an odd farm at your elbow, another nudging you at a distance, perspective playing tricks with proximity, until with help from the skyline of towers, turrets, campaniles, that dot the horizon as the way winds upward, I am suddenly on foot in the thick of things, walking with awkward step on streets paved in brick to the Osteria del Vicario.

I check into this hotel, a monastery in Boccaccio's time, where the cloister serves as a drinks terrace. My room is a cell with a window looking narrowly down a street. On a walk through the dusk, the only spots of light or life are from a proud little store that stocks the goods of half Italy, a café called Boccaccio, a small vintner selling chianti labelled with the writer's name and image. Wherever you look along the alleys of this precipitous city you glimpse postcards of Tuscan hills, the admixture of vineyards and olive groves selling you a distant prospect of Elysium.

Boccaccio spent the last seventeen years of his life within a hundred yards of where I now lie pretending to be a monk, having eschewed pyjamas in favour of a dressing gown as glum as a habit. His house, as next morning an inspection of the brickwork proves, was almost wholly destroyed in 1944, having survived six centuries unscathed. In the lower walls there are old bricks his eye must have caught. A pre-war photograph of his study is exhibited in the room the bombs hit. One side escaped, thus preserving the neo-classical fresco of Boccaccio at his desk, quill in hand, swathed monkishly in a species of dressing gown, interrupted in mid-sentence as if snapped by a paparazzo.

A wickerwork container behind him, all too similar to a waste-paper basket, contains scrolls of manuscript. A curious superstructure bears books. An inkwell has a stock of quills at its side. The general effect is to celebrate the utter tedium of writing as an occupation, reclusiveness as a way of life, gloom as a philosophy, and posthumous fame as a career. In this unspeakable fresco I see a man after my own heart.

The other rooms set the past in an opaque aspic. Whatever is preserved within them is at arm's length. Behind glass the cabinets contain editions of *The Decameron* in a host of languages unidentifiable by eye, facsimiles of early manuscripts that cannot quite be made out, smallish reproductions of all the known portraits of Boccaccio, medallions bearing his profile in plump bas-relief. He is obviously keeping himself well away from the stiffness of this shrine. Early chairs are so narrow as to numb the backside and so upright as to strain the spine, while instructing you on no account to sit on them. There is also, suddenly alive, a small selection of wood-soled medieval shoes with uppers elaborately worked and in case a pair of high heels, all unearthed in the bowels of Boccaccio's house when reconstruction started after the war.

I fix on these tiny feet. Boccaccio is taking very small steps in these shoes. He has a lot of weight to carry. He dislikes walking. It accounts for his rarely going anywhere. He has a bad ankle too. That is why he is reclusive. This shoe bulges at the back more than the other one does. They do not make a pair. Nobody told me he limped. He is in pain wherever he goes. The ache in his right ankle, unalleviated by drugs, rises up through his system until it reaches the brain, where its antics slowly give rise to an intolerable depression.

Giovanni thinks it convenient to believe it to be God's will, but he is not averse in his revisions of *The Decameron* to giving the Almighty yet another dig in the ribs which he hopes will not be noticed on the Day of Judgment. He places a wily trust in the Eternal Father's inability to understand the nuances of human irony. It's my own invention, he asks, isn't it? From this question of sacrilege he draws back, his toes tensing in the tiny shoes I am staring at. It comes to me, as if to him, that God first displayed his sense of the sardonic in the Garden of Eden.

For two pounds (as security they need a credit card) you are issued at the box office with a handy device with which to roam the town's remains. When activated by any button fixed to wall or showcase or palace, marked 'i' for information, this earpiece tells you in a foreign drone the background to whatever you are looking at. You also have a spiral booklet identifying with a photograph what the 'i' you have pressed tells you that you are

looking at. With any luck this network of modern communication will prove the hi-tech route to the truth about Boccaccio: a further passport to the man.

But the droning tone turns the open air didactic. Your brain
is in chains. The voice keeps forcing you to pause. It directs
your eyes one way only, tacitly forbidding them to stray. The
inner ear becomes dizzy with a scholarship as mangled in
narrative as the syllables are in accent. I feel resentfully in thrall
to that awful voice in the ear, until the moment of rebellion
comes in the church, when I want to hear not another word
about Boccaccio.

The church of St Jacob is very dark. It is a relief not to see
things at all clearly. I am forewarned by 'i' that Boccaccio is
buried within its gloom. Breathing easier, I slip the dratted
machine into my wet mac pocket. I am in the presence, or rather
the absence. The place where the original slab was laid fell victim
to the late war. A stone diamond marks the spot. Further west
from the altar lies a recent bas-relief, yet another of the none-
too-accurate images, more highly wrought than Boccaccio
would allow a sentence to be in one of his stories. Yet he
occupies the spaces of this church, beyond and below destruc-
tion. Here he is, under the floor, having already enjoyed in peace
a good twelve generations of progressive evanescence. I walk
companionably all over him.

This is his late city. As with a sniffer dog pulling on the lead, I
hunt for clues: a visual or two, details which Giovanni in
retirement might have added to a story in its final revision,
places that liven up one of his settings for undercover lust or a
display of power or a practical joke. Here is the Pretorio Palace,
the seat of Certaldo's government, the walls enamelled with

majolica coats of arms backed by strips of unrestored fresco, on which Boccaccio's passing eye alights.

By now the dog is straining at the leash. Windows look out on scraps of garden gone to seed, a few fruit trees long unattended. Here were all the plots fermented, all the gossip whispered, the rumours traded: sex stalked these corridors of power. The dog is now pulling hard enough to turn my ankle over. I am just about into viewing the palace as more or less certainly his location for that lewd tale about the Tuscan abbot who drugs the husband into apparent death to give excessive comfort to the wife who believes herself widowed, when a hammer starts hitting nails.

This sound comes from nowhere near the Middle Ages. In the now empty saloons of the Pretorio Palace, which once resounded to those mutters of betrayal and conspiracy, a number of young people are setting up an exhibition about poets. Working against time, they are tacking together modern bits and pieces, expanses of thin board in plywood frames looking gimcrack, with tools ill-handled, in order to hang art, pin up snaps, dangle pages of pretension in an over-explanatory wordiness that rings of propaganda. This may be art, but they are not craftsmen. Machines buzz out of control in waspish rage. Screwdrivers skew off the screw with shouts of dismay. The present reasserts its dominance, and my whole self, in precarious balance between then and now, scatters.

I cannot struggle back to the story. It has vanished as if it were untrue. In Certaldo the tension drains out. I have the sense of my subject escaping me if I try to chase him. He is playing hard to get. My instinct is to run away from this place to have any hope of finding it. With speed and address, my mind going before me, blind now to the beauty, I pack and pay the bill. Nothing more is to be found here now. The ghost of Boccaccio is far too subtle to be captured by persistence. Discoveries are made on the wing.

The vaunted Tuscan landscape, with only me dimly in sight, is veiled in swathes and sweeps of rain.

Meanwhile, behind the scenes of my solitude here at Santa Maddalena, the Baronessa is quietly at work arranging treats that seem distraction but end as serendipity. A Florentine hostess has asked us to lunch; I am preoccupied with the elusiveness of Boccaccio. As I rattle into Florence on the train, I brood over my three pioneers, at least the two younger of whom might have met on diplomatic missions to this city, which Chaucer visited for as long as six months in 1373, though Froissart mentions Chaucer, his sole reference, as an envoy in 1376. I still ache for my men to be captured alive.

All I have is an address in Florence that feels as unnerving as an assignation. I am about to be unfaithful. The ankle playing up, I get puffed looking for the Via San Spirito in airless canyons of alleys unmarked on the street plan. I keep debouching into long squares where churches bookend an acreage of unwalkable cobbles. A sweat steals into the armpits and springs to the brow. If asked, nobody Florentine or faintly resembling Boccaccio recognises either my accent or my urge to locate one of their smarter streets. I am in no fit state for luncheon when at last I fetch up at a palazzo sandwiched between similarly oppressive edifices.

Cross and hot, I walk up dark stairs into a family palace to find myself a guest of Bona Frescobaldi. Her triumph last night is all over Florence's morning newspaper which, true to principle, I have failed to read. She has outshone in jewellery, and no doubt in beauty, HM the Queen who happens to be honouring Rome with a state visit. All Italy is now gripped by just such a mannerly parade of diplomacy as when Chaucer turned up to attend on England's behalf an equally grand occasion. A few floors up the butler opens the massive door. He bows; chivalry is back. In a saloon a number of persons dressed more at their best than casually are at the gracious pastime of talk.

She has assembled a party of eight. Of course the apartments look different now from when Boccaccio marched his depression to and fro – every defile of a street hugging the Arno is a muddle of pasts – and an extra half-millennium of art has hung money from the walls or looms in marble, but the spaces are the same, the perspectives, the ceremonies of leisure. For an instant we are sharing centuries of that urge to refinement that sometimes seems (though not always) the best of what is human.

The windows of the upper saloon where we sip a white Frescobaldi wine overlooks a garden of tangled formality backed by a church local to Boccaccio's boyhood. A campanile soars. The bells boom through noon as nuts are downed and drinks drunk. I tingle. I am closer. Nothing is better for work than suddenly being compelled not to do it. With no help from me, indeed behind my back, Geoffrey has arrived in town on royal business. Jean might not be far away. We are all due for a reunion if only I can pin down Giovanni. The tall glasses are refilled with white wine to a tasteful minimum as we recline in chat on overindulgent upholstery. Florence is all of a sudden at the centre of all time.

We speak naturally, and as if it were natural, of how and why I am bringing together my trio of contemporaries here in Florence; I know with a lunge of high spirits who I am and therefore what I am doing. Again the mood of the room takes it for granted that Florence is at the heart of things, including my search. With manners as perfect as the occasion takes for granted, we move into a dining room as stuffed with art as a museum and a half, but also lived in. Masterpieces scale the walls to the mouldings; they look lived with. The luncheon, in a room suffused with sunlight as soft as if reflected by mirrors, is served by the soft-footed butler, and it feels like being alive. A mushroom risotto is as rich as impasto. A lashing or so of Frescobaldi chianti clears it off the palate. A veal stew thickly juices carrots and potato. More of the wine cuts it. The fruit salad to follow is a cornucopia no doubt echoed in a still life above my head.

The women present are those who survived the plague thanks to Boccaccio's stratagem of making them tell stories on the flight from Florence. They tell stories now with much gesture and verve. Their elegance of address and of dress is a pleasure to share; their company makes mine shine. There is every formality but every relaxation within it. Bona Frescobaldi's invitation to lunch with her whenever I am researching Boccaccio in Florence ceases to be a surprise when I judge her kind impulse to be an act of solidarity with Boccaccio; her family stretches back that long. Florence is still tiny, but still at the centre of things, loyal to the shadows of itself, but engaged in a plotty intimacy, call it gossip, unchanged in centuries of an independence almost arrogant from the rest of the known world. Abruptly, donated with grace, I have my freedom of its past. At our next lunch I shall meet Giovanni or be made an alderman of the city or speak Italian like a native.

★   ★   ★

The next diversion must be meant. Even I cannot resist a direct brush with art being created out of nothing here and now at the behest of a master on the spot.

In his mind's eye the Villa Mansi might once have provided Giovanni Boccaccio, as it now serves Bernardo Bertolucci, with a setting, a set. The villa stands grandly off the lanes above Lucca, and my hostess has secured us an invitation to watch the shoot and share the unit's lunch break.

Bertolucci's wife, Clare Peplow, is directing a version of the Marivaux comedy *The Triumph of Love*: a French play in English realised by Italians. Yet I am in no hurry for this plunge into media matters when I am not only clinging in spirit to the courtly manners of the Via San Spirito but also halfway back into the elemental crudity of time at Santa Maddalena. To my pleasure we get lost on the way to the villa, the Italians among us often stopping to ask the direction rather than read the map. Making contact with the locals, they claim, is more reliable than cartography. I am encouraged to think we shall get more lost.

I arrive at the old villa to find myself facing the tangles of my youth when movies were the hot language. At a glance there is the usual mix-up and mess that obtains on a film set: lamps burning you harder than the sun, cables snaking in and out of the tackle, the general air among the technicians of being as averse to creative activity as to physical effort. The villa is in rapid desuetude: flaking, fading, statues dissolving, ceilings still half-alive with fresco colour but not for much longer, upstairs floors caving in, a grand culture biting the dust in slow motion – the Renaissance beyond rebirth. The house is hemmed in by plantings of mixed trees, by now over the top, too high, the ornamental lake a fetid green, despite one or two fishing rods abandoned in it, awaiting an angler. The air of the past is heavier than usual, harder to breathe than the present.

I watch a stylish scene being shot in a salon. A lot of clatter precedes it, hasty whispers of advice to actors on their guard, machinery being clumped closer, the hiss of a camera on a track, shouts, time running out, at an unseen signal everyone poised for a take: action! Then: the silence total, the hour timeless, the focus precise, the fear palpable, rehearsed lines flowing new-minted – until: cut! Then again, and once again, and yet once more, then: print it! And tension relaxing, failure receding, time rushing back like blood to the head, eyes meeting, heads nodding, a hand touching a shoulder, a kiss. A moving image, long considered and agonised over, now awaiting development in the dark: lo and behold, the truth is in the can. Everyone pretends not to be heaving a sigh of relief. And breaks for lunch.

On plastic plates we eat well from a buffet of pastas, meats, salads. A small vaulted room for the privileged and names worth dropping is equipped with proper cutlery and bottles of Tuscan red. I am at one table with Bertolucci and sundry others. Her smile almost wider than her wide-brimmed hat, Clare is at another table with her sister Chloe who is married to Adam, son of the poet Al Alvarez, an Oxford contemporary of mine. Their two well-mannered little girls serve us with coffee. Here too is Saskia Spender whose grandfather Stephen I knew when living in France. Ben Kingsley the actor sits bald and remote at a lunch of his own, his back bulging out his name on the studio chair. A set-designer's perspective of false obelisks and topiary brighten up the deteriorating park.

I see new versions of the faces of old acquaintance. Adam's half-moon smile has an ancient origin in his father, as does his shuffle. A distant echo of Stephen flits across Saskia's face. Abruptly I am in a society far larger than local. On a foreign lawn, the weather beyond reproach, I am faced with visual proof of the contrariety of being terminally alive, of living at several levels. Even to enumerate these levels strikes my brain as a harrowing task, though all day they interweave in front of or inside me. I feel them perceptibly merging, as the afternoon warms up, into a single force that will somehow surely be the making of this headlong run from the media, this experiment in getting myself a life, this risk that is at once an escape and an escapade. I must put it simply. Otherwise I cannot think of it all at once. I have to repeat my phrases as if learning a language that has only just sprung to life.

I stand in the sun. Over there is a villa in dire need of repair. This sixteenth-century vision I am viewing from a nineteenth-century English garden running now to seed. The more important persons who are moving about this scene belong to Marivaux's eighteenth century. They are costumed to show off the graces of its famed wit. They are also my contemporaries. And any grace sharply contrasts with background figures in jeans who man cameras and lamps. The actors are there to impersonate someone else or embody some alien idea. They stay quietly absent between takes, as they think and will themselves into a past that is the lifeblood of today. Then, at a further level, on the fringes of the action, are the children, even grandchildren, of friends of mine with whom I am out of touch, men known in smoky rooms at Oxford or met in the shade of luncheons in southern France.

But all the above-mentioned threads are oddly reconciled by the presence of an admired director, this Bertolucci, whose talk at lunch idles and sweetens me into realising that I can never have enough levels to deal with. I feel the lure of being directed by Bertolucci. He cannot know he is drawing a good inner performance out of me, that in talking about masses of other matters – his communism, his Italy, his movies, his loves, his desire for sun, his opinion of the wine – he is pulling together all the strings that are about to bind the only package which at this minute matters most for me. In that second when he is sloshing out more wine, words pouring from his mouth, he is the multilingual stand-in for all three of my pioneers, a modern embodiment, as original as they are in pictorial language, in the hurry of his thought, in being alarmingly up-front and on the advance and shooting from the hip and achieving his own vernacular focus on the times he inhabits and being immoderately alive. He is Chaucer in his humour, Boccaccio in the clip of his narrative, Froissart in his aptitude for gossip. Yes, I will say when I am invalided home, I met Bertolucci.

All eight of the above levels (if I have counted them aright) I carry around with me. They are quite a weight on a warm day. I have to keep sitting down in the shade or resting my eyes on a distant clump of trees. I feel I am mentally juggling them, condemned to keep them in the air at all costs or my whole thesis will come tumbling down. I am still sagging under this burden of levels, not knowing where to put them, when it is suggested we take a quick look, on the way back to Santa Maddalena, at the open-air theatre in the Villa Reale, also in the hills above Lucca. My levels are relieved when it turns out to be closed, but Beatrice pulls rank with the janitor and we enter the formal gardens – suddenly to be ravished by an ordered Eden. If no apple tree is in sight, the lemons and oranges recede in a perfect lesson in perspective, the centre of each tree emptied by pruning so that fruit proliferates at the extremes. They too are art fruiting best under discipline.

Behind ramparts of clipped hedge we come upon the theatre.

It is made entirely of greenery. The hedges disclose the entrances. Holes in the foliage allow for lighting the play. The stage is a bank whereon the cropped grass grows. The area for the audience is a lawn similar in size to the space for the performers. You breathe green herein, evergreen, the resin of slow-growing verdure. It clears the mind as eucalyptus does the nose. And my mind at once falls upon it as a setting, not just for a drama or even a recitation from *The Decameron*, though the listeners might be held spellbound in the twilight, but for laying down the load on my ankle and, if necessary by declamation, sorting out the interplay of the plethora of levels that have been fevering me all day to the point of nervous collapse.

I need no human audience. I require only to be left alone in a playhouse of the imagination that can almost be heard growing around me, its murmur of myriad insects all the applause I want, milliards of leaves bristling in the breeze to cheer me on. What is more, this perfect layout has all the acerbic sense of the seventeenth century's tunnels of shadow to tease me out of excess, mock my pretensions, while adding yet another century to the day's interlock of eras.

In spirit this venue could be lent back to the *Trecento* if it needed it for my purposes. We can use what we like of the past for any reason we choose, should it lend me something I can repay. Here Boccaccio is at home too.

A party of Germans led by a guide armed with facts swarms in upon the theatre's silence. We flee, but not before recording it permanently on the film of the inner eye. A delinquent urge to pocket one of the nicely brought-up lemons is resisted, and then we are back in the car to Santa Maddalena after a day of amalgamating hints of what anyone interested in squeezing more juice out of living might want, if not too greedy.

I am back in the present, yes, but only from getting the hell out of it. Ready for home I am.

AFTERWORD

When I come back to England from Santa Maddalena a month before Christmas, plans have been set in train for an operation to be attempted on the ankle.

It is still an entity apart from the rest of me, so I am in two minds. If the surgery is a success, I shall be unwilling to part from an irascible old friend who, faults aside, kept me company during this adventure; if a failure, I shall be dominated for ever by its incurable pessimism. What's more, at the hospital in north London where several hours early I check in for tests, there is nothing to do but watch television. I feel I am betraying everything I have been up to, but it is no use: the beastly box is a drug against fear, a means of getting out of my mind without going out of it. Well, an anaesthetic.

So the general anaesthetic comes as a welcome relief when I am wheeled in, the surgeon's eyes in close-up watching it take effect as in a film involving torture. There can be little more like death than the slight high that precedes the moment of losing oneself completely. A second later I wake up, not surrounded by nurses, but alone, helpless in the grip of circumstance, the TV set on. I cannot distinguish between the realities, who is starring in what, whether the story about the ankle is on the world news, or what programme I am tuned to.

I find a doohickey and turn off the set just as the surgeon enters to present me with a complimentary video of my operation.

For the first time in my life I can really look inside myself for as long as fifteen minutes. It could be fame for the ankle. It is not only on tape but a star. The white coat also instructs me in how to spend my next few days: leg up higher than my head, as much rest as I like, exercises for the ankle to pain it into submission. All night I cannot sleep. The mind is abuzz with imagery from the year's trips, which through half-closed eyes I allow TV to assist, and like the condemned man I eat a good breakfast, still not knowing whether I shall ever walk again.

With a stick, but leaving behind his £800-a-night bed, Lazarus struts down to the car and, passing through a novel London glazed with pride and promise, I reach home, lie down and surrender to the media. If I am as yet too weak to hold a book, the bed is tumultuously counterpaned with newspapers, the set is eternally on; I switch channels with a maniacal mixture of relish and despair, ever hoping for a finer hour of drama, a comedy fit to make my ankle bone burst its sides, a commercial that will taunt me into a desire to acquire a bargain or possess a luxury: I am returning to human normality, if not to life itself.

So it is in bed, protected by those who love me, beyond interruption except by those invited, that I begin to learn the first of lessons from one or other aspect of this year-long caper. As the ankle snuggles on its high-kick pillow I am recuperating. I have earned solitude. I have steeled myself into becoming the one and only force that can invade my privacy.

A thought strikes me. In the story I told, I illustrated, if only to myself, how by bringing those three men and their time together in my own fashion I had digested them into myself, and here I was, thus and therefore, coming out with flying colours as an amalgam of them, full of affection for, understanding of, delight in, the media they cast the mould of: an old man transformed if not converted into a modern one on the make.

I also thought how banal was that conclusion, if spelt out as above. I mistrusted its instant appeal as a positive end towards which these pages had worked. It smacked of the slick. But it remained seductive, put as follows: we had to first resist, then adjust to, in the end embrace, the media, thus making them ours rather than letting them dominate our lives. Certainly we had to edit them, subject to scrutiny what we saw or heard, remember that their unconscious but most compulsive impulse was to undermine, corrupt or vulgarise, protect our children against the bag of sweeties offered by the media, put and keep the media in a constant perspective – so as to enjoy their excesses by shrugging them off.

This was an affirmative way to end up and well-rounded. It gave a kick to an old media hand like me. But it also let us off the hook, the implication of that acceptance being as follows: we have to smother in congratulations, rather than question or blame, the three men who started the process, for their rude, early, modern sense that the more people understood one another, and so helped one another, the better. And the best preparation for both achieving the understanding and giving the help was threefold: (1) sipping deeply at history, like Froissart, combining the alcohol of eyewitness and the mixer of commentary in equal measure; (2) falling for narrative fiction, so being drawn by the heartbeat rhythms of Chaucer deeper into the spirits of people different in mind from oneself; (3) filming with our eyes what we consciously saw, extending the range of our vision, a process aided by Boccaccio, whose stories were as crisp as screenplays. They all nudged us to get adult. They prolonged us.

So, waking up to yet another guiltless day in bed, trying to bring the fourteenth-century men and the twenty-first-century media together again in a partnership that leads further, seems in order, if only to keep my mind in. In fact I have been prescribed the media as medicines to keep the ankle quiet. Slightly off horizontal, a see-saw stuck with leg in the air and head on the deck, I can no longer distinguish between reality and dreams and media and past. They shift in and out of a numb mind, making up a story that seems at once to have no absolute meaning but to be of the utmost significance. Such is life.

The children visit dutifully to mock me. Dad is watching daytime television. Dad is draped in the *Sun*, wrapped in the *Mail*, buried in the *Telegraph*, suffocated by *The Times*. Dad's grasshopper mind is switching from soap to news to play to flick; Dad is tuning in to life's rich variety. At last he is giving up and becoming human and you have to respect him, but yes, Dad, this is really funny. They pretend to hide their grins behind hands as grubby as the jokes they are making at my expense. Only the helplessness of my invalid condition preserves me from further martyrdom.

Luckily they do not loiter in the sick room. They have better things to do, if not to think about. I watch them go with more love than relief. As children will in their teens, they make me look afresh at the idiocy of myself, as all this year did my three dear old friends from the past.

A NOTE ON THE AUTHOR

David Hughes is the author of many books including the novel
The Pork Butcher (winner of the 1985 W. H. Smith Literary Award),
a biography of Gerald Durrell and, most recently, the memoir
The Lent Jewels. A former film critic at the *Sunday Times*, he
was for many years chief fiction reviewer at the *Mail on Sunday*.
He lives in North Lambeth and East Kent.

A NOTE ON THE TYPE

The text of this book is set in Bembo. This type was first used in 1495 by the Venetian printer Aldus Manutius for Cardinal Bembo's *De Aetna*, and was cut for Manutius by Francesco Griffo. It was one of the types used by Claude Garamond (1480–1561) as a model for his Romain de l'Université, and so it was the forerunner of what became standard European type for the following two centuries. Its modern form follows the original types and was designed for Monotype in 1929.